Oriental Rugs and Carpets

Fabio Formenton

Oriental Rugs and Carpets

Hamlyn

London · New York · Sydney · Toronto

Translated by Pauline L. Phillips from the Italian original:

IL LIBRO DEL TAPPETO
© copyright 1970 Arnoldo Mondadori Editore, Milan

English translation © copyright 1972
The Hamlyn Publishing Group Limited
London · New York · Sydney · Toronto
Hamlyn House, Feltham, Middlesex, England

6th impression 1979
ISBN 0 600 02888 7

Text filmset by Filmtype Services Limited, Scarborough, England
Printed and bound in Italy by Arnoldo Mondadori Editore, Milan

Frontispiece:
Hans Holbein the Younger
The Ambassadors (*detail*).
National Gallery, London

CONTENTS

FOREWORD

Oriental carpets have, for centuries, been an outstanding example of those currents flowing between Eastern and Western civilizations which no international rivalry or historic struggles have been able to dam. Armed men, by sea and land, from the Bosphorus to the Pyrenees, have, from time to time and with varying degrees of success, played a bitter part in political and religious domination. No-one can deny, however, that Oriental carpets have decisively conquered the West on their own account. They, more than any other Oriental art-form, have shown themselves capable of becoming perfectly integrated into the stylistic and cultural structure of Europe. The reasons for this success lie in their ability to combine the functional and the ornamental. (It is not by chance that their history ranges from the tent of the nomad to the splendid palaces of the emperors.) They make our homes more comfortable, more welcoming and more beautiful.

Much has been written about Oriental carpets and this has given publishers opportunities to combine such writings into art books of great value. A new publication on the subject must, therefore, have, if not a justification, at least a precise motive, which can explain the opportuneness of a new contribution. It must be said straight away that, unlike many other, equally valid, works, this book does not treat Oriental carpets as exotic, exceptional and reserved for a few connoisseurs.

The book is divided into sections, the first of which sketches in the history of carpet-making, its beginnings and its spread. The next section contains illustrations of the most important types of historic carpets which can be seen in museums, a small collection of precious rarities so arranged as to reveal the continuity of traditional techniques and decoration with production, which is looked at more closely. The following section takes a closer look at techniques of manufacture and decoration, and supplies the reader who – for the first time, perhaps – is dabbling in the world of carpet-making, with the means of picking out the fundamental elements and of recognizing and evaluating a piece of work, from the point of view both of stylistic provenance and commercial value.

The nucleus of the book is a systematic list of the most important centres of Oriental carpet-making divided into five large geographical zones: Turkey, the Caucasus, Iran (Persia), Turkestan and Afghanistan, China and India. This catalogue is easy to consult because the centres are arranged in alphabetical order and because it is illustrated with maps of each region and colour plates of the most representative carpets and rugs. A register of the provenance, technical details and description of each type makes this collection a complete guide intended for anyone who, for whatever reason, is interested in Oriental carpets.

11

HISTORICAL
LANDMARKS

A REVOLUTIONARY DISCOVERY

Innumerable hypotheses have been formulated as to where and when the first hand-knotted carpets were made.

Some attribute the invention of carpet-making to the Egyptians, while others hold that the first carpet-makers were the Chinese. Yet others think that the earliest carpets were made by the Mayas. There is a foundation of truth in all these theories, since it is probable that many peoples, none of whom were in contact with the others, began to make carpets at about the same time.

On one point only are the various theories on the origin of carpet-making in agreement. This is that carpets originated from the need of nomadic peoples to protect themselves from the cold. They covered the earth floor of their tents with an article which, because it was softer and warmer than just animal skins, was more suited to their purpose. According to this theory, carpets had no pretensions to being an art-form at this stage and were only transformed into a work of art by a long, slow evolution culminating in a period relatively close to our own.

A recent archaeological discovery has, however, demonstrated that as long as twenty-five centuries ago, carpet-making had reached an extremely high artistic level. This discovery shows that, from the very dawn of their history, carpets had an artistic as well as a practical function.

THE PAZYRYK CARPET

A hand-knotted carpet was found in the Pazyryk valley in a tumulus dating back to the fifth century BC. It was in almost perfect condition because it had been preserved in a thick sheet of ice which had protected it for twenty-five centuries.

Late in 1929, a Russian ethnographic mission led by Rudenko and Griaznov began the excavation of five kurgan (tumuli), dating from the Scythian period. The tumuli had been discovered in the Pazyryk valley, in the Altai mountains, 5,400 feet above sea level, and some six miles from the border of Outer Mongolia.

In 1949, during the excavation of the fifth tumulus, a magnificent carpet came to light which today represents the most important piece of evidence in the history of Oriental carpets.

The Pazyryk carpet survived as a result of a series of fortunate circumstances. The kurgan where it was found was plundered, probably not long after the burial there of the spoils of the Scythian chief to whom it was dedicated. Fortu-

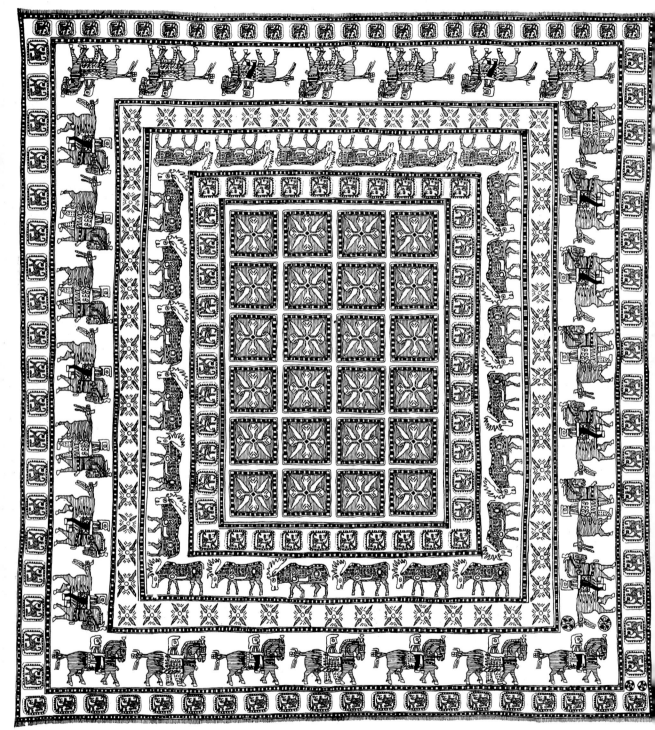

The Pazyryk carpet. In the lower right-hand corner are the two small circles the significance of which has been variously interpreted

14

nately, however, the carpet was in a secondary chamber along with the remains of some horses which had been buried with their master. Later, water filtered in and a thick sheet of ice formed inside the tumulus, which protected the carpet from the oxydization and crumbling of wool brought about by contact with air.

The Pazyryk carpet is of rare beauty and woven with great technical skill. The pattern is made up of two principal border bands flanked by 'guards' and a central field which is divided into twenty-four squares. The outer of the two principal border bands is decorated with a line of horsemen, seven on each side. Some are mounted, while others walk beside their horses. In the inside principal band there is a line of six elks on each side. The two external guards are decorated with a succession of small squares containing imaginary creatures, probably griffins. The guard between the horsemen and the elks is decorated with a figure like the cross of St Andrew, a motif which is also to be found in some Seichur carpets. The squares in the field design are also decorated with a similar motif.

The original colours used for this carpet are not known as they have almost completely faded away. The work of the Pazyryk carpet compares favourably with that of the best work from modern sources. There are about 270 knots to the square inch. It measures 6ft 7in × 6ft.

To whom should this carpet be attributed? Rudenko maintains that it is of Persian origin. It was, however, found thousands of miles from Persia and, therefore, very far away from the borders of the rising Achaemenian dynasty. Besides, since the Pazyryk carpet was found in a Scythian tomb, it could have been the work of Scythian nomads. In any case, some years after the Pazyryk carpet was found, Rudenko himself, during the excavation of a large Scythian

*The Pazyryk carpet (detail).
Note the changes which have
taken place in the colours*

15

tumulus discovered at Basadar, brought to light the remains of a knotted carpet of even finer work (330 knots to the square inch). This second discovery should dispel any doubts about the provenance of these carpets. In any event, there are many elements in the decoration of the Pazyryk carpet which confirm its Scythian origin.

Although the horsemen look decidedly Persian, it should be noted that the Scythians originally came from the north of Persia and were influenced by Persian costume. Besides, the head-covering, which comes down over the ears, was itself in use among the Scythians to protect them from the freezing winds of the steppes. Also, the elks shown in the smaller of the two main border bands confirm that the carpet was the work of a more northerly people than the Persians.

Another extremely interesting indication is the discovery made during the excavation of the second kurgan at Pazyryk. Among the belongings of one of the women was found an iron fork with splayed prongs. This unexpected find could not have been used for eating and archaeologists have failed to establish its purpose. The most likely explanation is that this strange fork was used by Scythian women to beat in the weft threads of the carpets they wove. To this day, this tool is used, without any significant modification, in the making of hand-knotted carpets (see page 51).

It should also be noted that the Scythians used to bury seven, or a multiple of seven, horses with each chief. If you look at the principal border band of the Pazyryk carpet, you will see that the horses are arranged in lines of seven.

The size of the carpet, and its special design structure, in which the uniformity of the central panel reduces it to a subordinate role in relation to the decoration of the main border bands, lend weight to the theory that it was a saddle-cloth. This hypothesis would confirm the notion that the carpet was made by Scythians who were, according to Herodotus, primarily horsemen.

Another theory is that this carpet was used for a game. This theory is based on the starting markers, four small circles to be found in the two main border bands.

Although the origin of the Pazyryk carpet may never be established with any certainty, the most likely theory is that it actually was made by Scythians or at least by nomadic Persian peoples living in northern Persia or Turkestan.

This hypothesis does not imply that the Persians were the first to make carpets. The fact is that the numerous carpets mentioned by Greek historians when describing Mesopotamian cultures, were also hand-knotted, contrary to the commonly held theory that they were embroidered.

The discovery of the Pazyryk carpet leads us, therefore, to the belief that, in a much more remote epoch than the sixteenth-century Imperial period, carpet-making had gone through an earlier, brilliant phase, in which a very high level of technique and decorative values had been reached.

CARPETS IN MESOPOTAMIA

If we analyze the history of the Middle Eastern peoples in the period preceding the fifth century BC – that is, before the date of the Pazyryk carpet – it is clear that the peoples of Mesopotamia possessed all the qualities necessary to sustain a brilliant phase in the early history and development of Oriental carpets.

The peak of this Imperial period must have been reached during the reign of Nebuchadnezzar II (605–562 BC), the last great Babylonian sovereign before the invasion by Cyrus in 539 BC. Carpets, in fact, have always played a special role in the evolution of the art of Middle Eastern culture. They were the first artistic expression of that culture and the symbol of the transition from a nomadic to a settled life. The latter opened up new artistic possibilities, and carpets were relegated to a secondary role. Indeed, the skill of the artisan and his artistic sensitivity were directed towards other products such as ceramics, pottery, sculpture, and textiles, which had become indispensable to the new mode of life.

When, after a centuries-long process of refinement, the art of one of these peoples reached perfection and passed from the instinctive to the more recherché, carpets, perhaps because of an atavistic need to return to tradition, once more assumed an important artistic role. The existence of the Pazyryk carpet presupposes that the people of Mesopotamia knew the art of knotting carpets. The Scythians had many contacts with Mesopotamian peoples, and probably learned from them how to knot carpets. One can also be certain that in the large cities of Mesopotamia the craft of carpet-making had reached a high artistic and technical standard.

CARPETS AND THE GREEK HISTORIOGRAPHERS

This thesis is supported by pictorial evidence and by the testimony of many Greek historians. One very interesting example which supports this thesis is an Assyrian floor found at Nineveh and dating from the tenth century BC, where the decoration is clearly derived from carpet motifs.

Many Greek historians confirm by their descriptions the existence and importance of carpets in Mesopotamian culture, and some even extend it to neighbouring cultures. Herodotus, for example, describes carpet techniques in Egypt, making it clear that in Egypt, by contrast with other places, there were men to attend to the making of carpets.

Xenophon, both in the *Anabasis* and in the *Cyropaedia*, mentions the importance of carpets in the life of Middle Eastern people and confirms the great value of some examples. Athenaeus describes the carpets of Sardis, the ancient capital of Lydia, which was conquered by Cyrus in 546 BC. The Greeks knew the carpets of Sardis best, probably because that city was for many centuries at the confluence of Greek and Oriental cultures and an important centre of trade. Quite apart from historical quotations, the importance the Greeks themselves attach to carpets confirms the value of this art. Aeschylus in the *Agamemnon* makes Clytemnestra spread precious carpets upon the ground to welcome her victorious spouse, and Agamemnon hesitates at first to step upon them, saying that only the gods were thus privileged.

CARPETS IN PERSIA

Once the presence of carpets in Mesopotamian culture has been established, it remains to determine when they were introduced into Persia and to examine their evolution in relation to the history of that country.

The epicentre of the craft of carpet-making is traditionally Persia and the history of the craft is linked to the history of Persia, sharing its development and fortunes. The other centres of carpet-craft of whose existence we have concrete proof from the Middle Ages onwards were manifestations of the work of isolated artists, though directly linked to the history of Persian rulers. The first group includes the ancient Caucasian carpets like the so-called Armenian ones, and to the second group belong carpets of the Turkish court period, coming from the workshops of Konya, the capital of the Seljuks, a dynasty which ruled Persia for a very long time.

CYRUS AND THE ACHAEMENIAN DYNASTY

It is very likely that Persian nomads knew the use of the knotted carpet even before the time of Cyrus, but almost certainly a true craft did not exist and the function of the carpet was more utilitarian than artistic.

At the time of the conquest of Sardis (546 BC) and Babylon (539 BC) the Achaemenian culture was still at its dawn. Confirmation of this is the fact that Cyrus, struck by the splendour of Babylon, refused to allow it to be sacked. It was probably he who introduced the art of carpet-making into Persia. It is said that the tomb of Cyrus, who died in 529 BC and was buried at Pasargadae, was covered with precious carpets.

THE SELEUCID AND PARTHIAN DYNASTIES

By contrast, there is no evidence to validate the use of carpets during the reigns of the other Achaemenian rulers, but there is reliable evidence of the existence of this art during the reigns of the two successive dynasties (Seleucid 312–120 BC and Parthian 170 BC–AD 226).

THE SASSANID DYNASTY (AD 224) – THE GARDEN CARPET OF CHOSROES (AD 641)

There are documents on the existence of carpets during the period of the Sassanid dynasty (AD 224–641).

The production of carpets in Persia is in fact mentioned in Chinese texts of the period. Moreover, the emperor Heraclius in AD 628 brought back a variety of carpets from the sack of Ctesiphon, the Sassanian capital. Among the spoils brought back by the Arabs who conquered Ctesiphon in 636 were said to be many carpets, among which was the famous garden carpet, the 'Springtime of Chosroes'. This carpet has passed into history as the most precious of all time.

It was made during the reign of Chosroes I (531–578), a Sassanid king known as Anushirvan (the Blessed). The Springtime of Chosroes was ninety feet square. From its exceptional size it seems probable that it was woven in the palace of Ctesiphon for which it was destined. The whole design represents a garden in springtime and was described by Arab historians thus: 'The border was a magnificent flower bed of blue, red, white, yellow and green stones; in the background the colour of the earth was imitated with gold; clear stones like crystals

18

gave the illusion of water; the plants were in silk and the fruits were formed by coloured stones.'

However, the Arabs cut the Springtime of Chosroes into many pieces which were sold separately. It is very difficult to establish whether this was a true knotted carpet or whether it was simply an embroidered tapestry. An interesting theory is that the Springtime of Chosroes, in spite of being made in a Persian court, belonged geographically to Mesopotamian carpet work, as Ctesiphon lay near to Baghdad on the banks of the Tigris.

PERSIA UNDER THE CALIPH OF BAGHDAD (661–861)

The Sassanid dynasty was followed by a long period during which Persia was under the domination, or at least the influence, of Arab caliphs. During the dominion of the caliphs of Baghdad (661–861), various Arab historiographers visited Persia and mentioned carpets as being among the products of that region.

These documents are not sufficient to establish that knotted carpets were made at that time in Persia. As a powerful local dynasty did not exist, it is very unlikely that high quality carpets were made, because until the eighteenth century these would have been part of the trappings of the court. On the other hand, the testimony of Arab historians confirms that the craft was not extinguished and that in addition to the carpets made by nomads, there were very probably some carpets of very real artistic value made.

It is interesting to note that the Qainat zone in the region of Khorassan was already known as a centre of carpet-making. This observation bears out the thesis which claims Qainat as among the most ancient centres of the art of carpet-making and the probable source of the most widespread motif in Persian carpet patterns: the herati (see page 71).

THE MINOR DYNASTIES (861–1037)

The dominance of the caliphs of Baghdad was followed by a period of no less than two centuries during which some Persian dynasties succeeded in obtaining a relative independence and in reigning over their own land. There is no certain information about the craft of carpet-making during these two centuries. One may suppose that, given the small importance of these dynasties, the art of carpet-making almost disappeared.

PERSIA UNDER THE SELJUK TURKS (1037–1194)

After the period of domination and control by the Arab Caliphates, Persia was conquered by the Seljuks, a Turkish people named after their founder. Seljuk domination was of great importance in the history of Persian carpets, the Seljuks in fact being very sensitive to all the arts. Their womenfolk were skilful carpet-makers, using Turkish knots (see page 56). In the provinces of Azerbaijan and Hamadan where Seljuk influence was strongest and longest lasting, the Turkish knot is used to this day.

19

In this period lived the two best-known Persian poets: Firdusi and Omar Khayyam. Although there was no reliable evidence of this, it is probable that in the provinces of Hamadan, and especially in Azerbaijan, knotted carpets were made which were of very high artistic quality, particularly in the first half of the twelfth century.

MONGOL DOMINATION (1220–1449)

In the latter part of the twelfth century Seljuk power gradually came to an end and Persia came under the domination of the Shah of Khiva who reigned over Kharezm, a central Asian state situated along the lower reaches of the Amu Darya river. This period was short, as in 1219 Persia was devastated by the hordes of Genghis Khan. The Mongols were a savage people and certainly knew nothing of any of the Persian arts. Very probably during this period carpet-making was carried on only by nomadic tribes. However, in time the Mongols came under the influence of the country they had conquered. The palace of Tabriz, belonging to the Ilkhan leader Ghazan Khan (1295–1304), who was the first Mongol leader to be converted to Islam, had paved floors covered with carpets. There is also further evidence confirming the presence of carpets in the period of Mongol domination, particularly during the reigns of the successors to Timur (Tamerlane) in Khorassan.

Among these, Shah Rokh (1409–1446) stands out. He contributed to the reconstruction of much that was destroyed by the Mongols and encouraged all the activities of the region. It is, however, certain that in this period carpets were decorated with simple motifs, certainly of a geometric type.

THE SAFAVID RULERS (1499–1722)

In the second half of the fifteenth century the Mongol dynasties gradually lost control of Persia. In the western regions they were superseded by the Turkoman tribe of the White Sheep, and their Emir Uzun Hassan set himself up in Tabriz in a palace where the paved floors were covered with carpets. At the same time, the last Mongol rulers were embellishing the palaces of Herat with carpets.

This was an important turning point in Persia's history because, after more than seven centuries of foreign domination, a national dynasty was in a position to gain power and take control.

In fact, in 1499 Shah Ismail I (1499–1524) drove out the White Sheep tribe and founded the Safavid dynasty. In the course of a few years, by means of a few expeditions sent out from Tabriz, Shah Ismail I succeeded in conquering almost all of Persia which thus came to be governed once more by a local dynasty. Liberation from the foreign yoke created a new ferment in the whole country and all Persian art saw a period of renaissance.

Shah Ismail was sensitive to this movement and facilitated the renaissance of the arts as well as gaining the sympathy of the people. The great miniaturists such as Bihzad and the disciples of his school, Sultan Mohammed and Mirek, lived at court with honours reserved for high dignitaries.

In the cities, craft centres were created for the manufacture of carpets. To these centres came the most skilled village craftsmen who, under the guidance of miniaturists, wove the knotted carpets for which Persia is famous.

The accession to power of the Safavid rulers is therefore of great importance in the history of Persian carpets. Moreover, it is from this period that the first concrete proofs of this craft are dated. In fact, about 1,500 examples from this period are preserved in various museums and in private collections. Shah Ismail was succeeded in 1524 by his son Shah Tahmasp, then a boy of twelve. Shah Tahmasp was devoted to, and a great patron of, all the Persian arts. His royal palace, first at Tabriz and later at Kasvin, was frequented by miniaturists and painters. It seems that Shah Tahmasp did not create a court workshop for carpets, preferring that this art should evolve contemporarily in all the centres of Persia, evidently under the control of artists and craftsmen from his court. In spite of the lack of an effective court workshop, the most beautiful examples of the Safavid period were made during his long reign. The best carpets of this epoch came from Kashan and Hamadan. According to a Hungarian ambassador to the court of Tahmasp, in this locality were made some splendid examples which the Shah sent as a gift to the Sultan Suleiman the Magnificent. Among the examples which have come down to us from the period of the reign of Shah Tahmasp are the carpet discovered in the mosque of Ardebil and the hunting carpet preserved in the Poldi Pezzoli Museum, Milan (see the description of these two examples and the other carpets of the Safavid dynasty, pages 30–43).

Shah Tahmasp reigned until 1576. After a turbulent period lasting for some ten years, Shah Abbas the Great (1587–1629) seized power. During the reign of this Shah, Persia went through a period of calm and national unity. Commerce and crafts prospered, intercourse was established with the great European states, and thus through gifts to rulers and ambassadors and through trade exchange, the Persian carpet penetrated into Europe and in a few years acquired great notoriety. In 1590 Shah Abbas moved his capital to Isfahan where, around a large square which served as a polo ground, he constructed a magnificent royal palace and two splendid mosques.

Shah Abbas also created at Isfahan a court workshop for carpets where skilled designers and craftsmen set to work to create magnificent specimens. These were almost always in silk and often contained gold and silver thread as well. At the death of Shah Abbas (1629) Shah Safi (1629–1642) came to the throne. He was succeeded by Shah Abbas II, Shah Suleiman and Sultan Hussein. During this period Persia found itself involved in various wars against the Turks, and consequently the arts underwent a progressive decline.

In 1722 the Afghans invaded Persia and occupied and destroyed Isfahan. This ended the Safavid dynasty and the court period of the Persian carpet.

FROM THE AFGHAN INVASION TO THE PAHLEVI DYNASTY

Afghan domination lasted about ten years and ended with the victory of a clever leader, a native of Khorassan, Nadir Khan who, in 1736, was named Shah of Persia. The reign of Nadir Shah (1747) lasted ten years, during which all the forces of the country were utilized in victorious campaigns against the Turks, the Russians and the Afghans. At the death of Nadir Shah (1747) there followed several turbulent years until a prince of the Luri tribe, Kherim Khan Zend, took power and had himself nominated ruler of the kingdom of Persia, establishing his capital at Shiraz.

During the reign of Kherim Khan Zend (1750–1799) the country knew some years of tranquillity but too few to recover from Afghan depredations and from the wars which followed. In this period no carpets of great value were made and the tradition of this craft was continued solely by the nomads and the craftsmen of the small villages.

After the death of Kherim Khan Zend, Persia went through a last period of disorder until Agha Mohammed (1786) took power and founded the dynasty of the Qajar which lasted up to 1925. They transferred the capital to Teheran.

During the reign of his successors, Fath Ali Shah and Nasreddin Shah, trade and craftsmanship regained their importance. The craft of carpet-making flourished once more during the last quarter of the nineteenth century because of the merchants of Tabriz who had begun to export to Europe through Istanbul. At the end of the nineteenth century, some European and American companies set up businesses in Persia and organized craft production destined for Western markets.

In 1925 Shah Reza, father of the present Shah, took power from the Qajars and founded the Pahlevi dynasty. Shah Reza encouraged the craft of carpet-making and created Imperial workshops where, to this day, specimens worthy of the great Persian tradition are made.

opposite page, above: *View of Kashan. Engraving made during the journey of the Chevalier de Chardin (seventeenth century)*

below: *Part of the royal palace at Isfahan at the time of Shah Abbas*

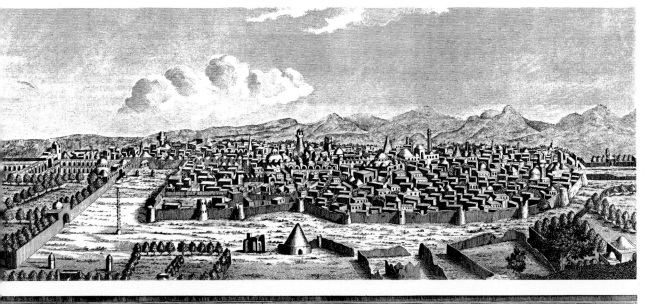

HISTORIC CARPETS

Before taking a closer look at historic carpets, it is necessary to formulate the criteria by which a carpet is classified as being historic.

Such a classification ought, perhaps, to be reserved for those rare fragments that have come down to us from antiquity. Mention has already been made of the Pazyryk carpet which dates back to the fifth century BC. There are, however, very few even fragmentary originals from really ancient times. Archaeologists from England, such as Stein, and from Germany, notably von Le Coq, have led expeditions in recent times to Turfan in Turkestan, and have had the good fortune to recover parts of carpets which, by reason of the analysis of the materials used and the decorative motifs employed, have been dated to around AD 500. Carpets from the mosques at Konya in Turkey may also be definitely classified as historic. Two of these, which were found in the mosque of Allah-el-Din at Konya, may be seen today in the museum in Istanbul, although they are in a very poor state of preservation. They date from the eleventh and twelfth centuries AD and provide a most authentic record of the medieval art of carpet-making. Their designs are still predominantly geometric, some details being of the type used in Anatolian carpets and others of that used in Caucasian carpets.

It is significant that carpets quite similar in design to some mentioned in this book appear in famous paintings of the fifteenth and sixteenth centuries. It is not without reason that the term 'Holbein carpet' is used to indicate the particular type of characteristic decoration which belongs to carpets from the fourteenth and fifteenth centuries. These carpets appear, for example, in the painting called *The Ambassadors* by Hans Holbein the Younger (see detail on page 6); in the *Virgin and Child* by Ghirlandaio; and in *St Anthony Giving Alms* by Lorenzo Lotto.

The world-famous Marby rug also dates from the fifteenth century. Details of this rug are given later in the book. It is in the Statens Historiska Museum in Stockholm and is thought to represent the phase when carpets passed through the gradual transition from geometric design – which was predominant in the Middle Ages – to the later, richly animalistic patterns.

Apart from these obviously rather rare examples mentioned so far, some two thousand specimens which have come down to us from the sixteenth and seventeenth centuries might also have the classification historic applied to them, were it not for the fact that no more than a couple of hundred of these possess any real value in terms of technique or decoration. In the last analysis, however, the term historic is narrowed down by two great practical difficulties. These are the problem of preservation and the rapidity with which a carpet deteriorates.

25

This depends, not only on external factors such as the wear and tear to the carpet caused by its very purpose, but also on the intrinsic factors inherent in the materials from which the carpet is made. Wool is a delicate material and is, by its very nature, subject to decay when in contact with the atmosphere, and eventually it reaches a point where the organic substance of which it is composed finally disintegrates.

In the review of historic carpets which follows, consideration is given to their artistic merit and, in addition, the opportunity is taken to offer a complete historical profile.

TURCO-EGYPTIAN CARPET   *Österreichisches Museum, Vienna*

PROVENANCE   A rare specimen which almost certainly came from the Sultan's workshop in Constantinople, founded by Egyptian craftsmen towards the end of the sixteenth century. It is at present on show in a most beautiful collection of carpets in the Österreichisches Museum in Vienna.

TECHNICAL DETAILS   The carpet measures some 17ft 9in × 8ft 6in and has Persian knots with approximately 205 knots to the square inch. The warp is yellow silk, the pile is also silk and the weft threads are of red wool. Twelve colours are used, including red, green, blue and yellow for the background, and various shades of green, blue, brown and yellow, with black and white, for the decoration. Because of the use of silk, the type of decoration and the various colours used, this rug looks completely different according to the angle from which it is viewed. Also, the amount of light transforms the colour values. It is, on the whole, in a good state of preservation, but one part of the field is very threadbare and has been repaired in several places (see detail of the field in the illustration opposite).

DESCRIPTION   The decoration is divided into four equal parts, each of which includes a quarter of the central medallion and half of one of the two medallions situated above and below the central one.

The decoration is composed of a succession of geometric motifs (especially octagons, but also stars, rosettes, triangles and rectangles) which are, in turn, filled with stylized plant patterns. The central medallion is made up of a great eight-pointed star-shape formed by a square and diamond combined. Within this large octagon may be seen two other shapes, picked out with different background colours.

The border is formed by a very large central band and five guards, two outer and three inner.

The decoration of the central band shows no sign of the geometric forms of the field, simply a tracery of red and blue stylized plant shapes on a green and yellow background.

PROVENANCE   This rug, which owes its name to the place where it was found, comes from the church of Marby (Jämtland) in Sweden.

It is not known exactly in which period this rug was made but, according to most experts, it belongs to the first half of the fifteenth century. This dating is confirmed by similar rugs which appear in fifteenth-century paintings, such as the *Virgin Enthroned* by Fra Angelico (1387–1455) and the *Annunciation* by Carlo Crivelli (1430–1493), the latter painting housed in the Städelsches Kunstinstitut in Frankfurt. Moreover, there is a comparative study by Flemming on the Marby rug and the fifteenth-century rug in the Berlin Museum from which it appears that the decorative structure, the techniques employed and the goat's-wool fibres of the two specimens are practically the same and that they may therefore be attributed to the same period if not to the same workshop.

It is not clear how this rare specimen came to be in Sweden. Various different hypotheses exist as to its place of origin. As a rule, its provenance is given as being generically Asia Minor, but the construction and design of the rug lead to a more specific attribution to the Caucasus.

TECHNICAL DETAILS   The Marby rug, which measures about 4ft 9in × 3ft 6in has Turkish knots at 50 knots to the square inch. The warp, weft and pile are of wool. According to analyses carried out to establish the place of origin of this specimen, the warp threads come from Tibetan goat's wool. The weft threads are red, as in many Caucasian specimens, and those which make up the pile are very thick as is usually the case with most Caucasian carpets.

The rug is in a fairly good state of preservation even though it was cut into two parts which have now been sewn together again. Because of this, a small central part of the rug has been lost between the two great octagons which form the main decoration.

DESCRIPTION   The rug has for its decoration two great octagons of equal size bordered by a typically Caucasian version of the Greek-key motif known as the running dog. Inside each octagon the decoration is composed of a highly stylized tree achieved by a skilful handling of the Greek key which can also be found in the decoration of the border. Among the branches can be seen two stylized birds which are also composed of Greek keys.

The border is cramped by comparison with the main body of the rug (this, too, is a characteristic of Caucasian carpets, and particularly those from Kazakh). It is composed of three bands. The central one is slightly wider than the other two. The simple decoration is formed by a succession of Greek keys.

The number of colours used is limited – yellow for the background of the main body of the rug; brown, white, blue and red in the motifs. If all the elements of this rug are taken into account – the octagon, the stylized animals, the Greek keys, the border and the colours – the similarity to Kazakh carpets is clear.

THE ARDEBIL CARPET

Victoria and Albert Museum, London

PROVENANCE   This specimen, at present on show at the Victoria and Albert Museum, is probably the best-known of all the carpets kept in the world's museums. It became known as the Ardebil carpet because it was discovered in a mosque in a town of that name in north-west Iran where Shah Ismail I, founder of the Safavid dynasty, is buried.

The carpet was brought to England in 1893 by Vincent Robinson who acquired it in Tabriz from the German house of Ziegler, one of the first firms to organize the craft of carpet-making in Persia. The Ardebil carpet is famous, not only for the beauty of its decoration and the advanced techniques used in its manufacture, but also because it bears an inscription and date which have enabled experts to establish the period and place to which should be attributed all the carpets of the early Safavid period. In a small rectangle set at the extreme edge of the main field of the carpet are the words:

I have no refuge in the world other than thy
threshold. There is no protection for my head
other than this door.
The work of the slave of the threshold
Maqsud of Kashan, in the year 946.

This inscription means, first of all, that we know the precise year when the Ardebil carpet was finished. By applying the method for changing a date in the Muslim calendar to one in the Christian calendar (see INSCRIPTIONS AND DATES on page 75) we obtain 1540. In this year Shah Tahmasp was on the throne and had already transferred his capital from Tabriz to Kasvin.

This transfer is extremely important in the search for the place where the Ardebil carpet was made. Indeed, one has to exclude Tabriz because, in 1533, it was invaded by the Turks and, in consequence, Ardebil to the north-east of Tabriz found itself isolated. On the other hand, there is no evidence of craftwork at Kasvin, one of the few centres where carpets were never made. Therefore, only the town of Kashan remains. This hypothesis is supported, not only by the name of the donor, Maqsud of Kashan (it is more likely in fact that the name inscribed on the carpet was the donor rather than the craftsman), but also by many other testimonies of the period. The Chevalier de Chardin, who visited Persia in the sixteenth century, left a document which is considered to be the most authoritative on the usages and customs in Persia at that time. De Chardin wrote 'In no other place in Persia are more cloths, velvets and carpets made than in Kashan.' Moreover, in 1601 Sigismund III, King of Poland, sent the Armenian merchant, Muratovitz, to Persia to order some carpets. Muratovitz, after a long journey through Turkey, Tabriz and Kasvin, ordered carpets at Kashan. Apart from these arguments and evidence, there is another point which positively confirms that this carpet, like the others from the early Safavid period, came from Kashan, namely the knot used. At Tabriz the Turkish knot was always used while these carpets are made with the Persian knot, the only one known in Kashan.

TECHNICAL DETAILS   The Ardebil carpet is just over 38ft long and about 17ft 8in wide. The Persian knot is used, at 345 knots to the square inch. The warp and

The Ardebil carpet: the central medallion

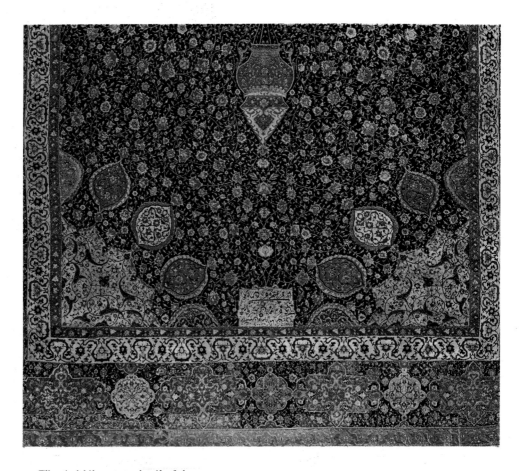

*The Ardebil carpet: detail of the
border with two corners*

weft are of fine yellow silk thread and the pile in close-cut wool. The state of
preservation is fairly good: repairs have been carried out using the wool from
another carpet found at Ardebil. Thirteen colours are used, including various
shades of blue, green, red, grey and yellow, and black.

DESCRIPTION   Against a field richly decorated with an interlaced pattern of
floral motifs there stands out a very beautiful central medallion which is the
most conspicuous part of the whole carpet. The medallion as a whole takes the
form of a sixteen-pointed star. From the two central points, on the vertical axis
of the carpet, hang two lamps. This detail of the design, together with the total
absence of human and animal figures, confirm that the carpet was intended
for a mosque. The four quarters of the field are each decorated with exactly
one quarter of the central medallion. (See illustration on page 31.)

The border is composed of a principle band in the centre and three guards,
one outer and two inner. The central band is decorated – as, in fact, is the whole
of the carpet – with the cartouche motif, typical of very many miniatures.

PERSIAN HUNTING CARPET
Poldi Pezzoli Museum, Milan

PROVENANCE   This carpet also, like the Ardebil carpet in the Victoria and Albert Museum in London, bears an inscription in the weave along with the date of its manufacture. The figures are not very clearly legible, with the result that there are two opposing interpretations: 929 of the Hejira, which is the equivalent of 1523; and 949 which is the equivalent of 1543. The second of these two dates would appear to be the most likely. In any case, this carpet, too, was one of the group of carpets belonging to the early Safavid period, because of its decoration and, in particular, because of its technique, and must have come from Kashan. This specimen was donated to the Poldi Pezzoli Museum in 1922 by Queen Margherita. Before that, the carpet was in the Villa Reale at Monza. No-one knows how it was imported into Europe.

TECHNICAL DETAILS   The hunting carpet in the Poldi Pezzoli Museum measures 18ft 9in × 12ft. The Persian knot is used at 270 knots to the square inch. The warp is made from double silk threads, the weft being in rather dark coloured cotton and the pile is in double wool threads. The carpet is in a fair state of preservation and was restored during the reign of King Umberto I of Italy. However, the carpet had been cut into seven pieces and resewn. Sixteen colours are used – black, white, pink and various shades of grey, red, yellow, blue and green.

DESCRIPTION   The field of this carpet is similar to that of the Ardebil carpet in London with the same background and tracery of flower designs, although in this carpet the decoration is more primitive and schematic. By contrast with the Ardebil, on the background of this specimen there are scattered mounted huntsmen and their prey. This type of decoration reveals the influence of the stylistic models of the Persian miniaturist school, in particular of the court miniaturist, Bihzad. The central medallion, one fourth of which forms an equal part of each of the four quarters, is also reminiscent of the Ardebil carpet, without being as sumptuous. The border, which is composed of a large band framed by two guards, is extraordinarily beautiful owing to both the originality of the design and the combination of colours. The cartouche in the centre of the carpet bears the following inscription:

It is by the efforts of Ghiyat Uddin-e-Jani
that this renowned carpet was brought to such
perfection in the year 949.

This carpet in the Poldi Pezzoli Museum is certainly one of the most beautiful specimens still extant. The colours enhance the harmony of the design (see pages 34–35).

above and opposite: *Hunting
carpet (Poldi Pezzoli Museum,
Milan)*

HUNTING CARPET

Österreichisches Museum, Vienna

PROVENANCE   This carpet, too, belongs to the first Safavid period. Its place of
origin was probably Kashan as for the hunting carpet in the Poldi Pezzoli
Museum and the Ardebil carpet in the Victoria and Albert Museum. It would
seem that this carpet may have arrived in Vienna in about 1696 and was a gift
from Peter the Great to Leopold I.

TECHNICAL DETAILS   This very rare specimen is made entirely of silk. The warp
and weft threads are of yellow silk and the pile is also of silk, dyed in about
twenty different colours.

The knot density is very high – 840 to the square inch. The Persian knot is
used. The basic colours used for the background and the border are salmon
pink, wine, pale green and white and, for the decoration, various shades of
green, blue, grey, green and gold.

The particular characteristic of this carpet lies in the fact that parts of the
figures are embroidered in silver and silver-gilt thread. On the whole, the carpet
is in a good state of preservation. There are some repairs to the central medallion
and in the border and there is a dark stain in one corner. The colours have
changed and faded rather more than in other specimens from the same period.

DESCRIPTION   This carpet is displayed in the Österreichisches Museum für

37

angewandte Kunst in Vienna. Of all the carpets from the first Safavid period, this one more than any other shows the great influence which the court miniaturists had on the decoration of carpets in the Persian court period. Most experts maintain that the sketch for this carpet was designed by a miniaturist, Sultan Mohammed, a pupil of the celebrated master, Bihzad. In this case, the carpet, which retains the characteristic flat decoration, could only have been made in the period between 1540 and 1555, the year when Sultan Mohammed died.

The structure of the decoration is the classic one: a central medallion, one fourth of which appears in each of the quarters, while the border is composed of three bands – a central, more important, one and two guards. The field is decorated with figures of mounted huntsmen, armed with swords, lances and bows who pursue and slay a variety of animals – leopards, antelopes, lions and wolves.

The eight-pointed central medallion is decorated with phoenixes and dragons which denote Chinese influence. The most beautiful part of the carpet is, without doubt, the central band of the border. Against a wine-coloured background appear figures side by side alternately seated and kneeling, amid a tracery of flowering branches. The decoration is completed by various species of birds placed among the branches (see page 37).

THE TREE CARPET   *The Philadelphia Museum of Art, Philadelphia*

PROVENANCE   The provenance and period of this specimen have provoked much discussion among various Western experts who have not, however, succeeded in coming to an agreed conclusion.

Some say that the carpet goes back to the first half of the fifteenth century and would therefore have been made during the reign of Shah Rokh, son of, and successor to, Tamerlane. In this case, the carpet would have had to come from the north-east of Persia, because Shah Rokh resided at Herat, and not from the north-west where continual battles took place with Turkoman tribes. Other experts believe that the carpet belongs to the second and third decade of the sixteenth century. In this case, it would have been made between the end of the reign of Shah Ismail and the beginning of the reign of Shah Tahmasp. The second theory, which seems the more likely, places this specimen among those of the first Safavid period. The carpet shown here forms part of the Williams Collection and is displayed at the Philadelphia Museum of Art, Philadelphia.

TECHNICAL DETAILS   This carpet is 17ft 3in long and 17ft 9in wide. The Persian knot is used, with 250 knots to the square inch.

The warp is made of white cotton threads, the weft of a double cotton thread and the pile of rather short-cut wool.

Eleven colours are used: red for the basic colour of the ground, white and various shades of blue, yellow, brown, red and green for the motifs. The carpet is in a rather poor state of preservation as it is very worn and has been repaired in various places.

38

DESCRIPTION The decoration of the field is related to the traditional flower decoration of garden carpets. The whole field is covered with rows of cypresses, alternating with flowering shrubs and boughs arranged in a harmonious symmetry of line.

The border is composed of three bands, two smaller with one main one in between. The latter is decorated with an unusual and harmonious interlacing of arabesques, identifiable by the three different colours used, yellow, blue and red. All the motifs are picked out on a background of midnight blue.

The two guards are decorated with rosettes interwoven in a garland, a motif which may be found in almost identical form in specimens of recent manufacture.

PERSIAN PRAYER RUG *Metropolitan Museum of Art, New York*

PROVENANCE This specimen is to be seen in the Metropolitan Museum of Art, New York, and belongs to a group of Safavid rugs made chiefly in the second half of the sixteenth century.

TECHNICAL DETAILS The dimensions are typical of prayer rugs: 5ft 6in × 3ft 3in. The Persian knot is used and the knot density is very high – 660 knots to the square inch.

The warp is composed of a combination of fine double cotton threads. The weft is wool, as is the very close-cut pile. The central part of the niche contains silver. Ten colours are used: red, white, yellow and green for the background with white, black, various shades of yellow, green, blue and orange for the motifs. The rug is rather worn and has undergone a number of repairs.

DESCRIPTION The decoration of the field is composed of the niche and two quarters. In these are verses from the Koran, each on a different coloured background. The niche is outlined along the sides and base by the inner guard of the border and, along the upper part, by a white band with more inscriptions from the Koran.

The inside of the niche is decorated with a floral motif where the silver is very conspicuous. In the upper part of the niche is a lozenge with an inscription from the Koran.

The decoration of the border is somewhat original in that it is divided into two parts. The lower one has a light background with the classic floral motifs of the Persian carpets of this period. The upper part also has a light background with a transcription of verses from the Koran.

40

'POLONAISE' PERSIAN CARPET *Österreichisches Museum, Vienna*

PROVENANCE This rare seventeenth-century specimen, on display in the Österreichisches Museum für angewandte Kunst in Vienna, comes from central Persia and, in all probability, from Kashan.

Like other carpets of the same period, and with the same characteristics, this one is known as a 'Polonaise' carpet because of a curious misunderstanding. A collection of these specimens was exhibited in 1878 at the Trocadéro in Paris by Prince Czartoryski of Warsaw.

Because they did not know where the carpets came from, the Parisians, seeing the coat of arms which appeared on each of them, christened them 'Polonaise' carpets.

TECHNICAL DETAILS This carpet measure approximately 6ft 6in × 4ft 6in. The Persian knot is used with 180 knots to the square inch. The warp is of cotton and the weft is a combination of three threads, two of dark cotton and one of red silk. The pile is of silk. As well as the normal weft threads there are also silver and silver-gilt threads. These are a technical and decorative characteristic of this class of carpet. There are twelve colours used in this example, all in light shades – green for the central field, red for the border and, for the motifs, salmon, black, white and dark grey, as well as various shades of blue, green, yellow and red.

The carpet is in a fair state of preservation; there are no large repairs but it is very threadbare.

DESCRIPTION The fascination and fame of the 'Polonaise' carpets are due to the originality of their decoration, which is completely different from that of other Persian carpets of the same period.

There is no rigid pattern composed of a central medallion and four quarters. The various areas of the field are distinguished solely by changes of colour. The decoration is of the floral type, but executed in a primitive style, with no excessive attention to detail. The characteristics of the example reproduced here correspond to these special features.

The border, however, although in keeping with the character of the whole decoration, shows its Persian or, to be more precise, Kashan origin.

Of the two guards, the outer one is decorated with a motif formed by a triangle and a diamond with a common vertex while the inner one has a motif of rosettes and garlands. The central band has a simple decoration made up of a herati border design in an original, primitive but at the same time pleasing interpretation.

The three motifs which decorate the border of this specimen are also to be found in modern Kashan carpets.

These carpets have always been much appreciated in Europe where others also still exist. There is an important collection of them in the Residenzmuseum in Munich.

INDIAN PRAYER RUG

PROVENANCE   This rug, now exhibited at the Österreichisches Museum in Vienna, comes from the north of India. It was made in the second half of the seventeenth century, probably during the reign of the Moghul ruler, Shah Jahan, a period which coincides with the height of Moghul culture.

TECHNICAL DETAILS   The measurements are 5ft × 3ft 6in. The Persian knot is used, with 440 knots to the square inch. The warp and weft are composed of silk threads, while the pile is of close-cut wool. Thirteen colours are used: white, black and various shades of pink, yellow, green, grey and blue. The rug is well preserved except for some faded patches and a repair along the central band.

DESCRIPTION   The pattern is the classic one for all prayer-rugs, that is, it has a central niche. Two small cypress trees flank the niche on two sides and share an outline with it.

The upper part of the niche is like a ceiling vault, formed by a succession of small arches surmounted by two quarters containing a floral decoration on a yellow background. The inside of the niche is decorated with a central flowering stem from which radiate flower-decked branches.

The border is even more clearly influenced by Persian art, both in structure and decoration. It is made up of six guards, three outer and three inner, and a main central band. The guards with a light-coloured background are decorated with a motif composed of a series of rosettes between which passes a garland of flowering branches. The guards with a dark background have a Greek-key design.

The central border is closely decorated with interlaced branches and flowers standing out against the dark colour of the background.

44

TECHNIQUES

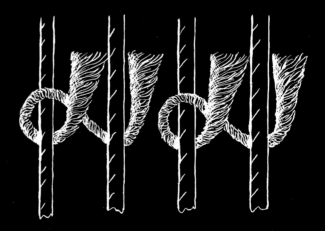

A special characteristic of all Oriental carpets is that they are hand-knotted. The fabric is composed of three parts: the warp, the pile, and the weft.

The warp is the combination of threads, usually of cotton, which are arranged vertically in parallel lines between the two ends of the loom. The pile is the visible surface of the carpet; it is made up of short threads, usually of wool knotted on to the warp. The knots are placed in rows across the width of the carpet, never along the length. The weft consists of one or more threads, nearly always of cotton, woven between one row of knots and the next.

LOOMS AND TOOLS

As we have said, Oriental carpets are made entirely by hand. Apart from the great skill and patience of the craftsman, all that their manufacture requires is a loom and a few rudimentary tools.

The looms may be divided into four types: horizontal, fixed vertical, Tabriz type vertical, and vertical with roller beam. The horizontal loom, the most primitive of the four, is very similar to the looms used by nomads to make the first carpets which were intended to take the place of animals skins on the floor of their tents. Carpets, in fact, answered both the aesthetic and functional needs of these tribes better than skins.

The horizontal loom consists of just two wooden beams between which the warp threads are stretched lengthwise. During manufacture, these warp threads are held in tension between the two beams by means of two posts tied to the ends of each beam and fixed into the ground. When the tribe wished to move on, all that was needed was to remove the two posts and roll up the made-up part of the carpet and the warp threads around the two beams of the loom. The horizontal loom was used solely by nomadic tribes.

The fixed vertical loom is also known as the village loom because it is used almost exclusively in small communities. It consists of two parallel round beams held up by two vertical supports. The warp threads are stretched between the two beams and the knotting of the carpet is always begun from the bottom. The craftsman works seated on a board hooked on to the rungs of a ladder fixed to the vertical supports of the loom. As the work proceeds, the board is raised from rung to rung so that the worker is always at the same height as the knots.

Carpets made on this type of loom are at most the same length as the loom itself, that is, no more than about nine feet. It is possible to make longer carpets by rolling the completed work around the lower beam and stretching a second

opposite page, above:
*Turkmen nomads working on a
carpet on a horizontal (ground)
loom inside a tent*

below: *Children working on a
carpet on a vertical loom*

this page: *Women hand-knotting
two carpets on vertical looms. The
cartoon may be seen in the
foreground*

set of warp threads above on the upper beam. This method, however, does not give good results and the two parts of the carpet often do not match. One development of the fixed vertical loom is the so-called Tabriz loom invented by the craftsmen of that town, which is now very widely used, particularly in the large carpet-making centres of Iran.

In this type of loom the warp threads run from the upper beam to the lower, passing below it and going back to the upper beam. This forms two parallel planes of warp, one in front and one behind. The carpet made on the front warp threads is passed under the low beam and up the back of the loom; at the same time, from the back the warp threads pass around to the front of the loom. This system enables a carpet to be made twice the length of the height of the loom.

The fourth type of loom with roller beams is a further development of the vertical loom. All the warp threads needed to make the carpet are rolled on to the upper beam, and the carpet is rolled on to the lower beam as it is completed. With this type of loom it is possible to make carpets of any length.

The tools used in the making of carpets are few and simple. They are a knife, a beater, and shears. The knife is used to cut the threads of the knot. It is entirely of metal and may have a hook at the end of the blade to assist in the formation of the knot. (This type of knife is used particularly by the craftsmen of Tabriz.)

The beater consists of a series of metal blades, the points of which are splayed to form a set of teeth. It is used to tighten the threads of the weft against a line of knots. The wide-bladed flat shears are used to clip the pile of the carpet.

THE RAW MATERIALS

There are three materials used in the manufacture of carpets – wool, silk, and cotton.

Wool and silk are primarily used for the knots which form the pile, and are more rarely employed as warp or weft threads, for which cotton is mostly used. Chiefly sheep's wool is used, but there is also a fairly widespread use of camel-hair, used for the most part in its natural colour. The employment of goat's hair is, however, much rarer.

As far as sheep's wool or possibly lamb's wool is concerned, the long-staple kinds are, of course, preferred. Wool from the shoulder and flank of the animal is best, while the poorer quality wool comes from the legs and belly. The quality varies from place to place, the wool from mountain sheep living at low temperatures being considered to be the best. Khorassan wool is also much appreciated. Wool obtained by combing the sheep's fleece in the winter and shearing it in spring is known as kurk, and is of the highest quality. Poorer quality wool is

opposite page, above: *Three different kinds of knife used by Persian craftsmen*

below: *Flat shears used for clipping the pile and two metal beaters designed for beating in the weft threads*

50

called tabachi and is obtained from the fleece of dead animals. Lime is used in this operation, the wool is stiff, dull and rough, and becomes lifeless when dyed.

Before being used, the wool must be carefully scoured in order to remove all traces of grease. The more it is washed, the purer and more vivid are the colours when it is dyed.

Among the most widely used qualities of wool are those spun by the nomadic Luri and Kurd tribes and used not only for carpets emanating from these two provinces but also for many carpets from western Persia. In some specimens with a wool pile, particularly those currently being produced at Qum and Nain, silk is also used to heighten the effect of the decoration.

Some rare carpets of a particularly sophisticated kind have a silk pile. These are usually carpets made to order. The best-known centre for this type of work is Kashan.

Cotton is used exclusively for warp and weft threads, although an exception to this must be made in reference to some Turkish specimens, in particular those from Kayseri where white cotton is used in the pile for the decoration of some motifs with a similar result to that achieved with silk.

Cotton is grown and spun in most of the places where the carpets come from. In antique carpets the warp and weft threads were nearly always in wool, or in silk in the specimens where the pile was silk also. Sometimes, for decorative reasons, silver, or silver-gilt thread was also used. In present-day manufacture, with the exception of nomad carpets which are entirely of wool, the warp and weft are in cotton and the results justify its use. In fact, cotton has less tendency to give and slacken than wool, and consequently when cotton is used, one does not find the unevenness typical of all-wool carpets. Besides, as cotton is stiffer than wool, the carpet lies better on the floor.

COLOURANTS

Next comes the matter of colours, that amazing artist's palette so typical of Persian carpet production. Dyeing is a very delicate process and is preceded by an alum bath which acts as a mordant. The thread is then immersed in a dye bath where it remains for a period ranging from a few hours to a few days according to the results required. Finally, it is put out to dry in the sun. Aniline was discovered in 1856, and its range of colours only reached Persia at the very end of the last century. Until the advent of these artificial colourants, dyers used nothing but natural ones, nearly all of them vegetable dyes. The exception to this among the most widely used colourants was the red obtained from the cochineal bug, an insect prevalent in India. Persian dyers became very famous over the centuries for their success in obtaining a seemingly inexhaustible range of colours from vegetable sources. Red, for example, was obtained not only from the cochineal bug but also from the root of the madder, a plant which grows wild in many parts of Persia. Other shades of red were obtained from other insects, while the pinkish-red and reddish-brown shades were the result of mixing whey with the normal red to produce a variety of shades of the same colour according to the amounts added.

Blue was obtained from the indigo plant, or more precisely, from the leaves of that plant. A very dark shade of blue, almost black, resulted from the use of the indigo which became encrusted on the inside of the fermentation vats. Yellow was obtained either from vine leaves or from a plant indigenous to the desert regions, or from weld which gives a beautiful saffron colour. Today, however, yellow obtained from weld is only rarely used, partly because it has become very expensive and partly because the more delicate tints are not perfectly fast. Green was obtained by mixing yellow and light blue which came from copper sulphate. Black came either from using the natural wool of black sheep or camels, or by dyeing grey wool with ferrous oxide found in the galls on oak trees.

Finally, the greys and browns were derived either from the natural colour of the wool or from dyeing carried out with ingredients taken from walnut shells.

Two stages of the dyeing process.
Note the primitive utensils
employed for this work

The use of ferrous oxide had the inconvenience of weakening the pile. In several old carpets, one can see where the black areas have become very worn and this creates a curious relief effect. This defect can also be seen in the green areas because of the use of copper sulphate. The creation of the colours by means of natural dyes is therefore very dependent upon the competence and skill of the dyers. The type of mordant and the hardness of the water used also have their effect. The water at Tabriz, for example, gives a certain dullness to the dyed wool. When, however, between the last decade of the nineteenth century and the beginning of the twentieth century, artificial colourants (the whole range of aniline colours) made their appearance in Persia, dyers abandoned the old traditions in favour of the much less costly new colours. Quality suffered and for a long time the fame of Persian carpets declined also, because the aniline colours gave tints which did not match and moreover had a tendency to discolour. The government itself had to intervene to preserve the quality by imposing very severe penalties against the importing and use of aniline dyes.

Persian dyers have been able to profit from the later progress in the chemical field and today, while the nomads tend still to use the natural colours exclusively for their dyes, town craftsmen and large workshops use many synthetic chrome-based colours which do not have the defects encountered in the aniline dyes. Chemistry also serves the creators of Persian carpets by providing the means of toning down the colours. This is called a reduction wash and is a chemical process which blends and softens the colours, making them more like the colours of antique carpets. It is a delicate operation which does not affect the durability and strength of the carpet, and this is all the more reason for purchasing carpets of a particular kind from a source where the processes used have been perfected from all points of view.

Often one finds a Persian carpet which at first sight appears to have a defect – or a rare effect according to one's point of view – but which is, however, a characteristic peculiarity. Certain designs or backgrounds begun in one shade of colour are continued in the same colour but in a slightly different shade, or simply with another colour. These discrepancies in colour are called abrash.

Abrash are, in fact, those variations of colour or shade which are particularly to be found in antique carpets. The presence of abrash is proof that the carpet was dyed with vegetable colourants. Indeed, with vegetable dyes it is very difficult to achieve two identical shades of the same colour.

KNOTS

As was pointed out at the beginning of the chapter, hand-knotting is the essential characteristic of all Oriental carpets. The knots used are of two different kinds: the Turkish or Ghiordes, and the Persian or Senneh.

The use of Turkish or Persian to distinguish the two different types of knot avoids confusion because these terms refer to the areas where the type of knot is mostly used. The Turkish knot is prevalent in Turkey and the Caucasus. The Persian knot is used mainly in Persia (although oddly enough, in the town of Senneh which gave its name to the Persian knot, it is the Turkish knot which is mainly used for carpet-making).

Dyed yarn left out to dry in the sun

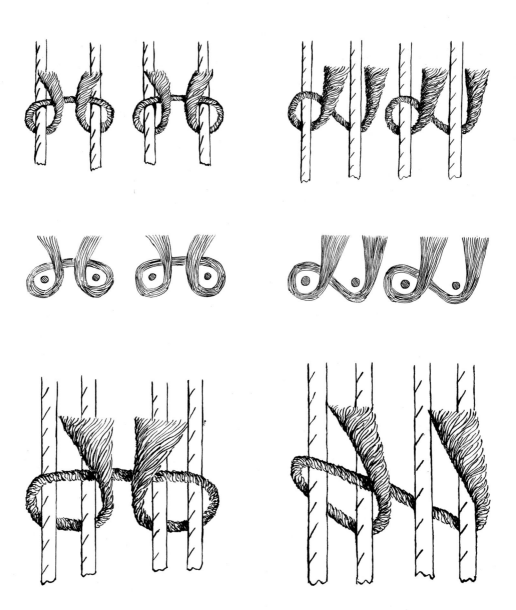

left, from top to bottom:
The Turkish or Ghiordes knot.
The same knot seen in section.
The jufti, or double Turkish knot

right, from top to bottom:
The Persian or Senneh knot.
The same knot seen in section.
The jufti, or double Persian knot

In the Turkish knot the yarn is taken twice around two adjacent warp threads and the ends are drawn out between these two threads (see sketch on opposite page). In the Persian knot the wool thread forms a single turn about the warp thread. One end comes out over this thread and the other over the next warp thread (see sketch on opposite page). By parting the pile of the carpet, it is possible to see a line of knots and determine whether Turkish or Persian knots were used.

With Turkish knots two ends come out on top of the knot, while in Persian knots one comes out at the top and the other is at the side.

THE WARP

As explained at the beginning of the chapter, the warp is the combination of threads stretched between the two extremities of the loom, around which the knots which form the pile are tied. Warp threads are usually of cotton. In nomad carpets the warp is of wool. The warp can be of silk in those rare carpets which are made solely of this material. The fringes of the carpet are the ends of the warp threads.

THE WEFT

The weft is formed by the thread or group of threads situated between one line of knots and the next. The weft is of cotton, wool or silk according to the material used for the warp.

The function of the weft is to hold the knots in parallel lines and to strengthen the fabric of the carpet. In most carpets the weft consists of two threads, one loose and one tight, which are woven across the warp after each line of knots. The weft threads are beaten in against each row of knots with a comb beater.

KNOTTING

A carpet is always begun at the lower edge with the selvedge. A certain number of weft threads are woven across the vertical warp threads so as to form a stout edging which will keep the carpet intact, prevent fraying and keep the knots tight. When the selvedge (which contains no knots) is finished, the knotting of the woollen pile threads on to the warp begins. Each piece of wool is fixed on to two adjoining warp threads in accordance with one of the two main techniques, Turkish or Persian. It is obvious that the price of a carpet depends on the time it takes to make, and, basically, upon the number of knots it contains. It is for this reason that over-hasty and at times cunning craftsmen use an unorthodox knotting technique. The practice of double-knotting called jufti (see sketch on page 56) is, for example, common. This double-knotting means that the piece of wool which should be knotted across two warp threads is knotted across four.

This technique diminishes the value of the carpet by reducing the density of the pile, thus making the decorative motifs less clear.

All the work of knotting is done by hand by a trained and swift craftsman. On average, a good craftsman can make from 10,000 to 14,000 knots in a day. This is a tremendous amount of work, even though the resulting piece of carpet may seem modest in size. Consider, however, that to make a medium quality carpet (at about 160 knots per square inch) and measuring about six feet by nine feet at a rate of 10,000 knots per day takes a good five months, and that in a whole day's hard work the carpet grows by less than an inch across the whole width. If the same carpet had a knot density of only 32 knots to the square inch, however, it could be finished in a month.

After each knot is tied, the carpet-maker pulls about $2\frac{3}{4}$ inches of the wool he has used away from the knot in a downward direction. This not only tightens the knot but also determines the direction of the pile. It is, in fact, a characteristic of Persian carpets that they appear different from different points of view and according to the way the light falls on the pile. Thus, when one wants to lay a Persian carpet in a room, it is important to try it out in different positions. Often a change of position can achieve a truly astonishing change of effect.

When he has finished a row of knots across the whole width of the warp, the weaver passes the weft thread in and out of each of the warp threads. Generally there are two weft threads between each row of knots, one tight and the other loose.

The pile is given its first cropping after four or six rows of knots have been made. (Sometimes, however, each row is cut individually.) The ends of the knots are kept fairly long (about $2\frac{3}{4}$in) whilst knotting is in progress. The final cropping will not take place until the carpet is finished. Specialized craftsmen are used for this work as it is a very delicate operation and one which gives the final touch to the work. As a rule, very fine carpets are cropped very close, while a deeper pile is left on carpets with a lower knot density because if these carpets were close-cropped the poor quality of the fabric would be revealed. The kinds of cropping differ according to custom and the demands of the market.

Nomads, for example, tend to retain a thick pile: the town craftsmen to crop it while the American market, which has a powerful influence on present-day Persian production, demands carpets with a fairly deep pile.

The miracle which attends the birth of every Persian carpet begins therefore at the knotting stage. Millions of differently coloured knots are patiently aligned one against the other to form the patterns and motifs – sometimes geometric, sometimes floral – but always full of imagination and style. Among the nomads, colours and designs often grow instinctively out of the basic tradition. There is no pre-ordained plan – just a general idea which takes into account the shape of the carpet to be made, the symbols which are to appear on it, and the colours available. All the rest is imagination, whim, skill and the innate creativity of the nomad.

In the cities, however, both in family workshops and larger concerns, the carpet is born of a precise project prepared by specialized artists who create the design on a squared cartoon on which each square represents a knot. When the carpet is to be made by one person on his own, the cartoon is fixed to the loom at the worker's eye level. When two or more people are concerned in the task, one of them reads aloud the number of knots of each colour. If you visit a Persian village, it is not at all unusual to hear an endless, monotonous chant coming from a house, '. . . one red knot, two blue knots, three red knots . . .'. This is the voice of the head of the family working at the loom with his son, one beside the other, with half a carpet each. At a rate of a few seconds per knot, the carpet grows like a great mosaic in which each knot corresponds to a tessera. In workshops where there are many workers, the weaving is led by the ustad (master) who superintends the entire manufacture of the carpet and is personally responsible for the most important parts of it.

The carpet is finished as it was begun, with a selvedge. When the last line of knots is finished, weft threads are interwoven with the warp threads so as to form a firm finish.

The surplus warp threads on each end of the carpet are used for the fringe which can be twisted or more often knotted. When the carpet is removed from the loom, it is given a final cropping and is then washed. The point of the wash-

Young woman working on a floral carpet. The rolled-up cartoon which serves as a pattern for the work may be seen attached to the loom

ing process is to remove the stiffness from the carpet and to restore the wool and colours to their full purity. The carpet is then spread out to dry in the sun and this is the last test of colour fastness.

SHAPES

Carpets are made in many different dimensions to meet the demands of the Western market. There are, however, particularly in parts of Iran, traditional forms due both to the local use of carpets and the various sizes of loom. The principal forms are:

QALI The literal translation of qali is carpet, although this name is used solely for carpets of large dimensions, i.e. 7ft 6in × 11ft or more.

DOZAR – SEDJADEH – KHALICHEN These three terms are used for carpets approximately 5ft–5ft 6in × 8ft–8ft 3in in size. Sedjadeh and dozar are interchangeable. The etymology of sedjadeh is dubious; dozar, however, means a precise measurement (do = two, zar = a Persian measurement correspond-

60

opposite page: *Carpets being washed in running water. The washed carpets are then laid out to dry in the sun*

left: *Carpets arranged in accordance with ancient Persian custom*

ing approximately to 4ft 2in). Two zar corresponds in fact to the length of these carpets. The term khalicheh is usually reserved for carpets of this size but of very high quality.

KELLEGI OR KELLEY AND KENAREH   These terms refer to two long types of carpet. The kellegi is the largest (approximately 6ft–8ft × 12ft–24ft) and the length is usually twice or three times the width. The kenareh is about 3ft 2in–4ft 10in × 10ft–24ft.

These two unusual shapes are due to the special arrangements of carpets used in Iran, i.e. a large central carpet, two very narrow side carpets laid beside the length of the central one and, finally, a fourth carpet arranged horizontally across the top of the other three and as long as the combined widths of these three carpets. The etymology of kellegi and kenareh confirms this particular arrangement: kellegi is derived from kelley which means head (head carpet), and kenareh is derived from kenar which means side (side carpet).

ZARONIM   In this case the etymology of the term is linked to the length of the carpet: one zar and a half (4ft 2in × 2ft 1in); nim in Persian means half. These are, in fact, carpets measuring approximately 4ft–4ft 4in × 6ft–6ft 3in.

61

PUSHTI OR YASTIK   Pushti, a Persian term, and yastik, a Turkish term, indicate the smallest rugs, about 2ft 3in × 3ft 6in. Pushti and yastik both mean cushion in Persian and Turkish respectively.

COMMERCIAL ORGANIZATION

Carpet-making in Persia is closely related to the commercial organization which takes care of the collection of the carpets. These may be carpets woven by the nomads which they sell when they pass through the bazaars of the cities, those produced spontaneously by country craftsmen, or town craftsmen who do their work to order, or those produced in the big centres.

The names of the carpets are always directly connected with their origin so that the carpet is both colloquially and technically classified by the name of the

A corner of the bazaar in Teheran

place of origin. If the carpets, however, have been woven by nomad tribes they usually bear the name of the tribe and sometimes the name of the geographical zone where they were made.

DECORATION

DESIGNS

Oriental carpets can be divided so far as design is concerned into two main groups: carpets with a geometric design and carpets with a curvilinear design, known as floral carpets.

Briefly, the difference between these two groups may be summarized by saying that geometric carpets are the expression of a particular style while the floral ones are an expression of art. In fact, geometric carpets reflect the style of particular craftsmen or tribes who made them, while the floral carpets arise from Islamic art and have, over the centuries, gone through the same evolution and changes as other expressions of that art.

GEOMETRIC DESIGN CARPETS

Belonging to this group are all the carpets decorated with linear elements composed of vertical, horizontal or diagonal lines. The design on the whole is simple and often formed by a repetition of the same motifs. Carpets with geometric designs are for the most part those woven by nomadic tribes, but geometric designs are also used in some small Anatolian, Caucasian or Iranian villages where, because of poverty and the distance from important centres, the decoration of the carpets has remained primitive. The first carpets had geometric designs, while the first specimens with floral designs only go back to the beginning of the sixteenth century.

The motifs of the geometric designs are, to all practical purposes, passed on by word of mouth. This detail facilitates the attribution of a carpet to a particular tribe or place of origin.

CARPETS WITH A CURVILINEAR OR FLORAL DESIGN

The beginning of the Safavid dynasty also marks the rise of the craft of Oriental carpet-making. The carpets woven by the nomads and peasants did not suit the refined taste of the Safavid rulers so there arose, especially during the reign of Shah Tahmasp (1524–1576), the first craft centres where floral-design carpets were made. Nomads and peasants were transferred to the towns and there, under the control of masters became engaged upon the richly decorated carpets which in a few years were to set the seal of prestige upon Islamic art.

Floral carpets, like the rest of Islamic art, reached the height of their beauty during the reign of Shah Abbas the Great. This high point of the floral carpet lasted until Persia was invaded by the Afghans in 1722, about a hundred years

A typical example of a geometric design

opposite page: *A typical example of a floral design*

after the death of Shah Abbas. Only during the last few decades of the nineteenth century was there a renaissance of the craft and from then on a high level of quality was maintained, in spite of the fact that the enormous increase in production very often led to a deterioration in the execution of this work.

The major difference between nomad work and that of the craftsman consists in the development of the function of the master designer, called ustad in Persian. In fact, while the designs of nomad carpets were passed on by word of mouth or grew out of the imagination of the person who made the carpet, the design of the floral carpet was drawn on a cartoon and meticulously reproduced by the skilled artisans. The work of these weavers was thus reduced to a simple manual task, whilst the ustad who designed the carpet and chose the colour got the artistic credit. The ustads in their turn belonged to various schools of design, of which those of Kerman and Teheran merit particular mention. In Teheran marvellous cartoons were designed which were suited to various production areas.

MOTIFS
The decoration of Oriental carpets consists of motifs which are much alike and which may be found with some frequency in specimens from different localities. These motifs may be divided into three groups: field motifs, border motifs, and decorative motifs.

FIELD MOTIFS
For the most part these are repeating designs used to decorate the whole field of the carpet. The best-known motifs are:

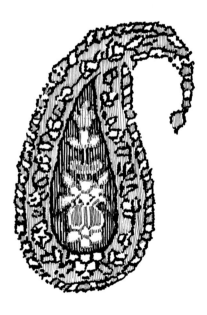 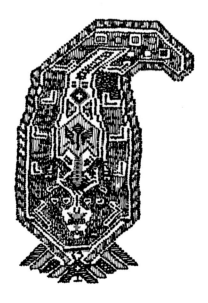

BOTEH

The boteh, known also as the almond or Kashmir design, is one of the most widely used motifs in Oriental carpets. Its shape is that of a drop of water with the upper part turned to one side.

Opinions on the geographical source and origin of this motif differ greatly. It seems, however, that the boteh design came from the Seraband region and that it was used at the beginning in the Mir carpets. This hypothesis is confirmed in some measure by the fact that this motif is also known by the name boteh mir. The origin of the motif lends itself to much conjecture. Some see in the boteh an almond, others a fig, and still others see a pine cone. The most likely hypothesis, however, is that the boteh motif is linked to the shape of the cypress tree.

The boteh is usually small in size (2in–8in) and is arranged in diagonal or perpendicular lines to cover the whole field. This motif is used in very large numbers of carpets and, according to the provenance, may be stylized to a greater or lesser degree and executed in straight or curved lines. The best-known areas where the boteh motif is used are Seraband, Mir, Kerman, Kashan, Senneh and Qum, and Shirvan and Derbent in Caucasia.

GUL

The gul, which in Persian means rose, is the basic decoration of almost all Turkestan carpets. This is the well-known octagonal shape which decorates Bukhara carpets and which is described in a section devoted to that locality. The origin of the motif is not certain. It is, however, interesting to observe that octagonal-shaped designs are also quite frequently to be found in other Oriental carpets, particularly those from Turkey and the Caucasus.

The gul is produced in different ways according to the place where the carpet is made.

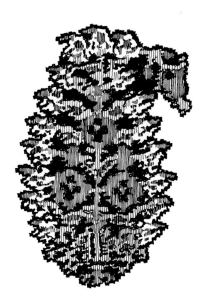

Three different interpretations of the boteh motif: the first on the left comes from a Kashan carpet, the second from a Senneh carpet and the third from a Mir

69

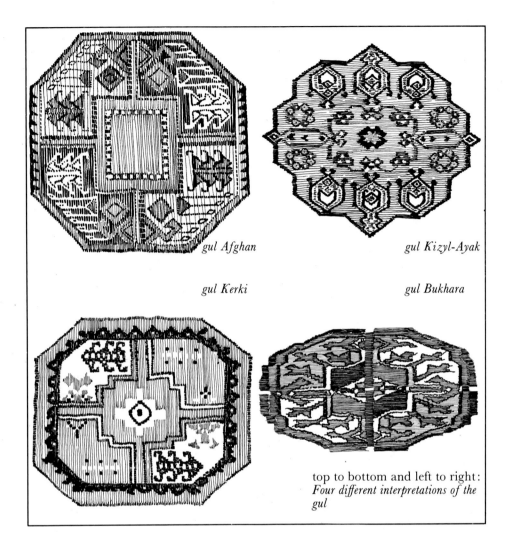

gul Afghan   gul Kizyl-Ayak

gul Kerki   gul Bukhara

top to bottom and left to right:
*Four different interpretations of the
gul*

HERATI

The herati is without doubt the motif which occurs most frequently in Oriental
carpets. It is easily recognizable because, in spite of the multiplicity of ways it is
used, the design is almost always unchanged. The herati motif is composed of
a central rosette enclosed in a diamond. At each point of the diamond are two
small rosettes, while along the four sides are four elongated leaves which faintly
resemble the shape of a fish. It is because of this resemblance that the herati
motif is also known as mahi, a word which means fish in Persian.

The herati originated in Khorassan and its name is derived from the city of
Herat which was for a long time the capital of that region. In carpets originating
in Khorassan, however, the central rosette of the motif is not enclosed in a
diamond. The herati is used particularly in north-west Persia: Bijar, Saruq,
Tabriz, Ferahan, and in some Caucasian regions.

70

*Two different interpretations of
the herati motif*

above: *The most common
interpretation in Persian carpets*

below: *The early herati motif in
which the rosette is not enclosed in
a rhombus*

JOSHAQAN

The joshaqan is formed by a succession of diamond shapes decorated with stylized flowers. This motif is used almost exclusively in carpets made in the village of the same name, and in some Kashan specimens.

HARSHANG

The harshang, which in Persian means crab, belongs to the group of motifs known as Shah Abbassi because they were created during the reign of Shah Abbas. Although it is Persian in origin, the harshang motif is used mainly in Shirvan carpets (see description under this heading).

MINA KHANI

The etymology of the name of the mina-khani motif is not clear. Mina is a

71

woman's name in Persian, and khaneh means house. It could be argued that the design of the mina khani, which resembles a field of flowers, was inspired by the garden of a house. The mina khani probably originated in Khorassan where it is also used in carpets of modern manufacture such as the Baluchi carpets made at Firdaus and Turbat-i-Haidari.

The mina-khani motif is made up of four flowers of equal size arranged in a diamond shape. A smaller flower appears inside the diamond so formed. This motif is repeated to form a complete ground decoration. The mina-khani motif is the most common decoration in Veramin carpets.

ZIL-I-SOLTAN

It would appear that the name of this motif is associated with a Persian dignitary who lived during the reign of Nadir Shah. In any case, the origin of the zil-i-soltan is fairly recent. The earliest specimens of carpets decorated with this motif are the nineteenth-century Teheran carpets as well as a few rare Ferahan and Malayer carpets of the same period.

The zil-i-soltan is composed of two vases, one above the other, decorated with roses and sprigs of flowers. Very often the figure of a bird is to be found between one vase and the next. The zil-i-soltan is used almost exclusively in Qum, Abadeh and Veramin carpets.

SHAH ABBASSI

This name is applied to a whole series of designs which came out of the golden age of Shah Abbas the Great. They are floral decorations, supposed to have been based on the lily, which were made famous by the carpets of that period. Nowadays these designs are most frequently to be found in Isfahan carpets.

They are recognizable in that they appear singly on the field of the carpet though they are generally linked to each other by vine tendrils, branches, and other plant decorations.

opposite page: *Harshang motif in a Shirvan interpretation*

above: *Mina-khani motif. Note the harmony of this composition*

below: *Zil-i-soltan motif as it appears in a Qum interpretation*

Zil-i-soltan motif taken from an Abadeh carpet

opposite page: *Two different interpretations of the herati border. The upper one, which is more formal, belongs to a Bijar carpet, while the lower more elaborate one comes from a Kashan*

BORDER MOTIFS

These motifs, as the name indicates, decorate the lateral bands of many carpets from different areas. The best-known motifs are:

BORDER HERATI

This motif is completely different from the field herati. It is formed by rosettes of flowers inspired by Shah Abbassi designs. They are placed in succession and branch out into flowered boughs of different shapes. The border herati, unlike the field herati, is interpreted in very different ways according to the place where the carpet was made.

The illustration shows two totally different variations: a very elaborate motif from the border of a Kashan carpet and a second, almost geometric variation, from the border of a Bijar carpet. The border herati is very widely used indeed and appears not only in carpets decorated with the field herati but also in other types of Persian carpet, particularly those from Kashan.

BORDER BOTEH

The border boteh is exactly the same as the field boteh. However, while the boteh is used on its own in the field decoration, it is used in the border in conjunction with other motifs which vary with the place of origin. On page 76 are illustrations of a Kashan border boteh, and a Kurdistan border boteh.

74

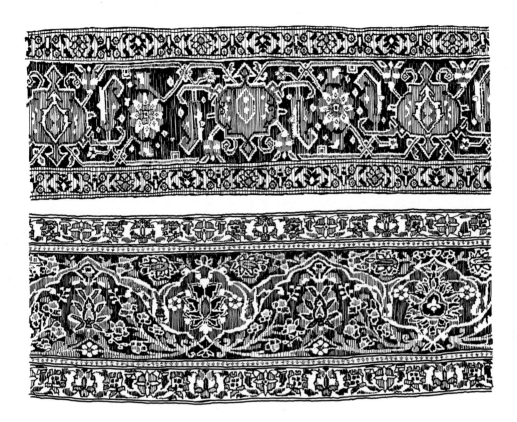

KUFIC BORDER

This border, which owes its name to its resemblance to Kufic script, is used in very many Caucasian carpets.

It should be noted that while Caucasian carpets often contain decoration of Persian origin, the border is almost always decorated with motifs typical of the district. The design on Kufic borders is always in white.

SERRATED-LEAF BORDER

This border is also typical of Caucasian carpets and is common in those with primitive designs, particularly Kazakh carpets. The design of this border is, as the name implies, made up of a succession of serrated leaves arranged obliquely.

INSCRIPTIONS AND DATES

The borders of many carpets also include an inscription containing quotations from the Koran, lines of poetry, dedications, and sometimes even an indication of the origin of the carpet and the period when it was made.

The dates are given according to the Muslim calendar. It may be useful at this juncture to mention that to find the date in the Christian era which corresponds to a Muslim year you should subtract from the Muslim date one thirty-third of the year number and add 622. The reason for subtracting one thirty-

opposite page, above and centre: *Two different boteh border motifs. The first, small boteh is highly stylized and has a limited decorative purpose (Kurdistan specimen). The second (Kashan) plays a more important decorative role*

above: *Serrated-leaf border. This type of border, which is highly formal, is to be found in various Caucasian carpets.*

opposite page, below: *Kufic border in a Shirvan interpretation*

third of the date in the Muslim calendar is that the Muslim year is some ten or eleven days shorter than our own. The 622 is added because the Muslim calendar numbers its years from the year AD 622, the year when Mohammed fled to Mecca.

For example, the famous Ardebil carpet in the Victoria and Albert Museum in London (see pages 30 and 31) which, according to the inscription on the carpet itself dates from the Muslim year 946, was made in about the year 1540 of our calendar. 946 divided by $33 = 28$; 946 minus $28 = 918$; 918 plus $622 = 1540$.

THE GUARDS

The borders of a carpet are always composed of one main band which is decorated with the principal motifs described above and guards which frame the main one. The guards also have their own specific decorative motifs which are common to carpets from different places. The following are some of these:

A motif composed of a succession of tiny quadrilateral shapes of different shades. This usually outlines the principal band of the border and is used in carpets from many areas including Shiraz, Ferahan and some parts of the Caucasus.

A motif made up of a line of rosettes linked by a garland of flowering branches. This motif is to be found in carpets from many areas and is interpreted in somewhat different ways, from the richly floral execution in Kashan carpets to the extreme linearization of Kazakh work.

A motif composed of a diamond and a triangle with a vertex in common. This shape is repeated with each figure joining the next to form a continuous pattern along the whole outside edge of some carpets.

DECORATIVE MOTIFS

Decorative motifs is a term which refers to those designs which are common to specimens from different places and which serve to complete the field and border decorations. These have been included in the description of the decoration relating to carpets from various places. The best-known are the eight-pointed star, particularly common in Caucasian and Bergama carpets, the rosette, various types of Greek key including the hooked variety known as running dog, and the swastika mostly used in Turkestan.

Three guards
from top to bottom: *Outside guard formed by a triangle and a diamond with a common vertex*

Guard formed by a line of rosettes linked by a garland
Guard formed by a succession of parallelograms

CARPET-MAKING
REGIONS

NOTE

Beside each map showing the places where carpets are made there are three symbols to indicate the principal characteristics of the carpets in question.

Symbol of a tent, i.e. of the nomadic life of the tribe who made the carpet on a horizontal or ground loom.

Symbol for carpets woven chiefly in villages and small communities by craftsmen using a vertical loom.

The criterion for the use of these symbols for each locality is the type of loom most commonly used. In the cases where both types of loom are equally used both symbols appear.

Turkish or Ghiordes knot.

Persian or Senneh knot.

This symbol indicates the yarn, wool or cotton, used for the warp and weft. Here, in the case of a mixture of fibres, the criterion is the yarn used for the warp because this is of more importance than the weft.

80

With the exception of Chinese carpets and a few specimens woven by India, the production areas of Oriental carpets are limited to certain Middle Eastern countries, of which Iran is the heart. The production areas can be divided into five large groups, as follows:

TURKEY
Turkish carpets include those woven along the shores of the Mediterranean and on the Anatolian plateau.

THE CAUCASUS
This area includes the vast region of the Soviet Union which extends from the Black Sea to the Caspian and is bordered in the south by the Iranian territory of Azerbaijan.

IRAN
The term Persian is applied to all the carpets woven in Iran, the name given in 1935 by Reza Shah to present-day Persia. Iran is the most important region for both quality and quantity of carpets.

TURKESTAN AND AFGHANISTAN
From this region come the carpets woven by the nomadic tribes who live in the trans-Caspian steppes as far as the mountains of Afghanistan to the edge of the Pamirs.

Far East: CHINA AND INDIA
With the exception of Chinese carpets, very few carpets come from the Far East.
  To this group may be added the carpets woven in Pakistan to designs originating in Turkmenistan.

TURKEY

ISTANBUL
Hereke
Bergama
ANKARA
Ghiordes
Kirshehir
Sivas
Izmir Kula Ushak
Mudjur
Kayseri
Melas
Ladik
Isparta
Yuruk
Yahyah

ANATOLIA
Yuruk
Mudjur
Kirshehir
Yahyah

ANATOLIA

PROVENANCE Under this name are grouped carpets from different places in the part of Turkey that runs from the central plateau to the Taurus mountain range in the south-east.

Although these carpets come from a very vast region and are woven both by nomads and by craftsmen from the many small villages, their common technical characteristics and similarity of decoration enable them to be classified under the generic name of Anatolia.

A closer analysis reveals two groups: Yuruk and Yahyah carpets woven by nomadic tribes; and Mudjur and Kirshehir carpets woven in the two villages of the same name.

TECHNICAL DETAILS Both nomadic and village carpets are primitive in technique and far removed from the system in use by craftsmen of the western coast of Turkey. The simple looms used may be either the ground or vertical type.

The pile is always made of wool, as are the warp and weft. Only rarely are the warp and weft of cotton.

The Turkish knot is always used and the number of knots per square inch varies from 40 to 100.

Because of the primitive techniques using small looms, Anatolian rugs and carpets are limited to small sizes. The most common measurements are 3ft 3in–5ft × 5ft–6ft 6in, or, in the longer shape, 3ft 3in–5ft × 8ft 4in–11ft 6in.

YURUK

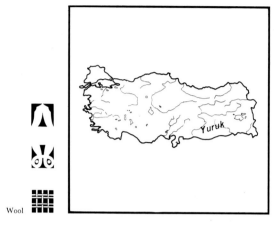

Wool

DESCRIPTION   These are the majority of what are known as Anatolian carpets. The design is mainly geometric and there is a vague resemblance, particularly in the borders, to motifs of Caucasian carpets.

The border is usually composed of a large band enclosed between two or four guards. Often the recurring motif in the wide band is made up of a succession of stars executed geometrically and divided into four equal parts.

The field design is frequently composed of a number of diamond shapes surrounded by a Greek-key design. This motif is enclosed in a series of hexagons of increasing size and varying colours. Often between the ground hexagon and the four corners there is the hooked Greek-key design known as the running dog. The corner decoration often consists of an eight-pointed star enclosed in an octagon.

Colour is one of the most predominant and pleasing characteristics of Yuruk carpets. These carpets, in fact, have very vivid but harmoniously combined colours. Yellow and violet are the predominant ones, with a hint of orange, green and midnight blue.

opposite page: *Typical Anatolian nomad carpet. In the decoration may be seen Caucasian motifs such as the serrated leaf in the border and the hooked Greek-key motif called running dog which outlines the central hexagon*

MUDJUR

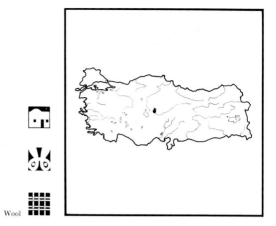

Wool

DESCRIPTION   These are nearly always prayer rugs. A special characteristic of Mudjur rugs is the width of the border, composed of a succession of bands decorated with geometric motifs, such as the star, rhombus and Greek key. The other part of the niche is often outlined with a simple Greek-key design which divides the upper part of the ground into two equal parts.

The central niche, nearly always self-coloured, is usually dark red or, more rarely, dull green or reddish-brown. Mudjur carpets are different from Yuruk not only in the fact that they are designed as prayer rugs, but also because of the different colour tones. The basic colours are the same, but the shades of the wool used are much less lively and brilliant.

opposite page: *Mudjur prayer rug decorated with clearly linear motifs. Note the two different decorations which form the border*

KIRSHEHIR

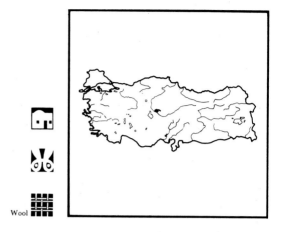

DESCRIPTION   Kirshehir rugs, woven in the town of the same name, are very similar to the Mudjur rugs, both because of the characteristics which they have in common with the Mudjur prayer rugs and because of the border, made up in the same way as in the Mudjur rugs with a succession of bands.

The major difference between rugs from these two districts lies in the colours which in the Kirshehir specimens are paler. The colours in the niches are paler by comparison with those of the Mudjur rugs. The dark red becomes cherry red, the dull green pea green, while pale blue and yellow replace the orange. Taken as a whole, Kirshehir rugs look more sober with a much more formal design.

YAHYAH

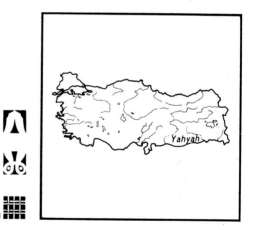

DESCRIPTION   The motifs of these carpets are very similar to those used in Yuruk carpets but differ from them in the linear nature of the execution. The Greek-key design around the diamond shapes disappears, the hexagons are reduced to one or two, and the border motifs are simpler. The design of the Yahyah carpets as a whole is even more reminiscent of Caucasian carpets. The colours are rather dark, but blend very well with each other as in Mudjur carpets. Yahyah carpets are often elongated in form, measuring approximately 4ft 3in × 9ft 10in.

Characteristic example of Yahyah work. The colour combinations are particularly pleasing

BERGAMA

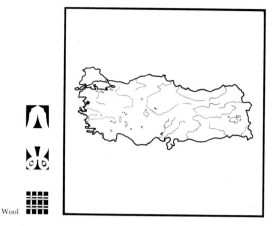

Wool

PROVENANCE   Bergama is a town in western Turkey about thirty miles from the Mediterranean coast.

The carpets from this area are, however, almost exclusively of nomad or semi-nomad origin, and owe their name to the city where they are sent for sale.

TECHNICAL DETAILS   As in all Turkish carpets, Bergama rugs use the Turkish knot. The knot density per square inch is rather low (33 to 80) and this is a characteristic common to all the carpets of Asia Minor.

The looms used in the Bergama area are almost exclusively horizontal. The warp and weft is in wool and it is only within the last few decades that cotton has been introduced.

The weft threads are almost always red and as many as three or four are used between the rows of knots, a characteristic by which to identify a Bergama. If, in fact, you look at the back of a Bergama rug, you can clearly see the red stripes formed by the weft threads. The fairly deep pile is always in good quality lustrous wool.

Another peculiarity of Bergama rugs is that they are nearly always almost square in shape. They are also almost always small in size, the usual dimensions being 2ft 7in × 3ft 6in, 4ft 3in × 5ft, and 5ft × 6ft 3in.

DESCRIPTION   The origin of these rugs is somewhat remote and is linked by affinity of design to sixteenth-, seventeenth- and eighteenth-century rugs known

opposite page: *Rare Ghiordes prayer rug dating from the end of the eighteenth century. The decorative motifs show French influence. The colours are typical of carpets from this area. (Pars Collection, Milan)*

90

by other names, such as the Holbein rugs named after the painter Hans Holbein the Younger, who portrayed some examples in his pictures; and the Siebenbürgen rugs which owe their name to the part of Transylvania where they were found but which almost certainly came from the Bergama area.

These are rugs of geometric and primitive design which also have an affinity with carpets from some parts of the Caucasus, particularly Kazakh. The dominant motif in a good many Bergama rugs is a large rectangle which occupies the central part of the rug. At the side may be seen small octagons and four-sided figures decorated with the eight-pointed star or stylized flower motifs. The designs used for Bergama rugs are so varied that rugs from the same locality may seem at first sight to be completely different. However, careful examination will reveal motifs which betray a common origin, such as the eight-pointed star, often enclosed in an octagon or circle. The octagons and squares are often outlined in a particularly brilliant blue. Azure, white and orange are the predominant colours for the motifs. (See illustrations on pages 106 and 107.)

Illustrated below is the central part of a typical Ghiordes border decorated with the characteristic motif known as janina

92

GHIORDES

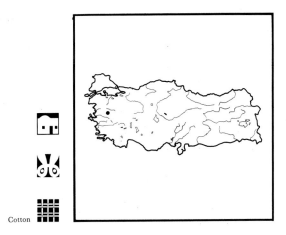

Cotton

GHIORDES

PROVENANCE   Town in western Turkey situated some sixty miles from the port of Izmir.

TECHNICAL DETAILS   Vertical looms, mostly small in size; warp and weft in cotton; two weft threads between one row of knots and the next.

The pile is a very close-cropped wool. The wool used is always best quality. In some Ghiordes rugs, undyed cotton is also used for the knots. The result is an opaque white motif which is outstandingly different from the rest of the rug. There are also Ghiordes rugs with a silk pile on a cotton backing. Some rare specimens are entirely in silk. The Turkish knot is used, with a density varying between 65 and 130 knots per square inch, the latter in silk rugs.

DESCRIPTION   Ghiordes rugs are the cream of Turkish manufacture. They are rugs of ancient origin and their design has affinities with the very beautiful and rare sixteenth-century prayer rugs.

Later production, as well as the completely modern Ghiordes rugs, are based almost exclusively on the prayer-rug theme.

The Ghiordes design, particularly in older and antique rugs, is closely and richly decorated. The border and the two rectangular cartouches placed in most specimens above and below the prayer niche, are decorated with stylized leaves, flowers, and fruit. This latter motif, known as janina, may be seen in the border of rugs made in the last century and even in modern ones. The janina motif is formed by a leaf set vertically between two round shapes to which it is joined by two stems. The round shapes are brightly coloured and resemble exotic fruit.

Another motif often used to decorate the border of Ghiordes rugs (particularly those dating from the second half of the nineteenth century and the twentieth century) is made up of a large number of small bands alternately light and dark in colour (ivory and red) and decorated with tiny flowers evenly spaced side by side.

The mihrab, the niche in the centre of the rug, is often supported by two columns, one on each side, while from the central part hangs a flower which often resembles an oil lamp. The niche is almost always outlined by a notched

93

or stepped border. Various colours are used for Ghiordes rugs. Firstly, these rugs must be divided into two categories: those over 150 years old which date from the court period, and those dating from the middle of the nineteenth century onwards.

The first group have rather drab colours. The niche is in dark blue or ivory or, more rarely, dull green. Also the number of colours used in the border motifs is limited and the shades used are quite light.

The second group, however, have vivid colours. The niche is often red and the border motifs stand out in brilliant hues. Among the predominant colours are yellow, orange, red and ivory. In spite of their vividness, the colours used in this group of Ghiordes rugs harmonize perfectly with one another. It is a play of colours which gives the rugs a very attractive quality. (See illustrations on pages 91 and 92.)

KULA

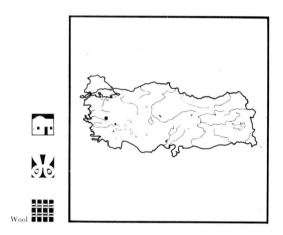

Wool

PROVENANCE   Kula, situated in the heart of western Turkey, is part of the province of Izmir. The rugs from this area are also woven by the semi-nomadic peoples living around Kula itself.

TECHNICAL DETAILS   Vertical and horizontal looms; warp and weft almost always in wool, more rarely in cotton; double weft thread between one row of knots and the next; pile in good quality wool, cropped fairly close; knot density from 53 to 80 per square inch.

Kula rugs, like Ghiordes and Ladik rugs, are small in size: 3ft 3in–4ft × 5ft 6in–6ft 6in. Some antique rugs were made in the longer form, 3ft 3in–3ft 6in × 7ft 6in–9ft 2in.

DESCRIPTION   Kula rugs, like most Anatolian rugs, particularly prayer rugs, have no special distinguishing motif and so are difficult to identify. To pick out a Kula prayer rug from a Ghiordes or other prayer rug one must first of all look at the techniques employed. The Kula almost always has a wool warp and weft and is light and limp, while a Ghiordes is stiff. The most commonly found types of Kula rugs are:

94

KULA-KURMUNDJU

DESCRIPTION Kurmundju means charcoal burner. These rugs are often made in very dark colours, dark blue for instance, which almost always covers the whole field of the rug.

The rugs are usually long and narrow, completely covered with a tightly packed design inspired by Turkish rugs of the sixteenth century. Colour is given to these sombre Kula-Kurmundju patterns by the violet, ochre and orange used in the floral motifs which decorate both field and border.

CEMETERY-KULA

DESCRIPTION Usually made up of large knots, Cemetery-Kula specimens are prayer rugs with the niche closely decorated with a motif composed of cypresses and small buildings. The motif is repeated vertically to cover the whole of the niche. The background of the Cemetery-Kula rug is usually cherry red with vividly coloured motifs. The origin of the name is not altogether certain. It was probably coined by a fanciful Western dealer who saw in the cypresses and other elements of the decoration the symbols of a cemetery.

Kayseri. The decoration of this specimen is obviously of Persian inspiration (Tabriz). The colours, raw materials and technique are, however, typical of the locality

Isparta. Specimen from the end of the nineteenth century. The decoration and the field colour are unusual and attractive. (Private Collection, Como)

KULA PRAYER RUGS

DESCRIPTION   These are the most common Kula rugs and even more difficult to identify because of their affinity with prayer rugs from other sources. Kula prayer rugs almost always have a small niche with so much decoration that the self-colour area is relatively small. Often the centre motif of the niche is a large tree of life while in other specimens there are two columns with a lamp in the middle from which hang flowering fronds which decorate the centre of the niche. A commonly found border is one formed by a series of bands, almost always in blue and white, decorated with small, regularly repeated flower motifs. (See illustration on page 99.)

LADIK

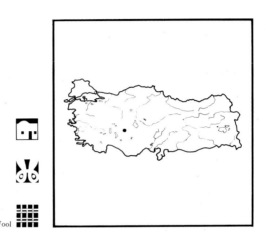

Wool

PROVENANCE   A small town situated in the heart of Turkey to the north of Konya.

TECHNICAL DETAILS   Looms are both vertical and horizontal and of small dimensions. The warp and weft are of wool, but in modern specimens cotton is also used. The pile is very beautiful because of its brilliance and the quality of the wool, and it is quite deep. The dimensions are small and regular: 3ft 6in–4ft × 5ft–5ft 6in. The number of knots varies normally between 60 to 120 per square inch.

DESCRIPTION   Ladik rugs are well known and, unlike rugs from other areas, are easily recognizable because of their unusual design. The border is usually composed of a large band framed by a series of two or three guards. In the wider central part a geometric motif enclosed between two lines forming a right-angle alternates with a stylized flower resembling a rose.

The guards are decorated with small stylized flowers joined together. The central part of the rug is divided into three areas: the niche, the spandrel and the lower section. The niche is nearly always self-coloured and is separated from the rest of the rug either by a straight line or a Greek-key motif, usually in white.

The spandrel is decorated with a stylized flower in the middle and by two motifs at either side which often represent ceremonial vessels. The lower central area is the characteristic part of a Ladik rug. Here there are three small niches oriented towards the lowest part of the rug, and each crowned with a very beautiful stylized tulip. Sometimes there are more than three tulips, because they emerge from both the inner and the outer vertex of the three niches. The predominant colours in these rugs are: dull red, ivory and olive green for the niche, and white, red, gold and beige in the motifs and border. (See illustration on page 101.)

MILAS

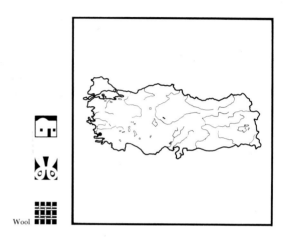

Wool

PROVENANCE   Town and province of south-west Turkey on the shores of the Aegean Sea.

TECHNICAL DETAILS   Vertical loom, occasionally horizontal. Warp and weft almost always in wool, occasionally in cotton; double weft threads between rows of knots. Medium length wool pile; somewhat limp feel. Knot density varies between 60 and 120 per square inch.

Milas carpets are in both the normal size for Turkish prayer rugs (3ft 6in–4ft × 5ft–6ft 6in) and in larger dimensions (5ft–5ft 3in × 7ft 6in–8ft 3in).

DESCRIPTION   As in the case of carpets from many other parts of Turkey and Anatolia, Milas carpets bear many different designs and so are rather difficult to identify. In Milas, many varied kinds of carpet are made as well as the classic prayer rug. These carpets, which are rare and much sought after, have as a common feature their range of lively colours. The predominant ones are lemon yellow, scarlet and bright blue, while the small motifs are in white and violet.

Milas prayer rugs are more easily identifiable because of certain characteristics which distinguish them from other Turkish prayer rugs. First of all, the Milas motifs are highly stylized and a vivid imagination is needed to recognize in them a flower or a tree of life.

Kula prayer rug, end of eighteenth century. (Pars Collection, Milan)

98

The niche in a Milas is particularly small in relation to the whole rug, and the upper part is characterized by two triangular identations. In the central part of the niche there is almost always a diamond from which spring either stylized flower shapes or eight-pointed stars enclosed in an octagon. Sometimes the diamond is joined to the base of the niche by a stem, a combination resembling the tree-of-life motif. The spandrel is decorated by a principal motif which spreads outwards from the centre.

The border is formed by a wide band decorated by diamond shapes alternating with highly stylized flowers. Beside this band there is often a narrow border divided by diagonal segments which form small rectangles, each of which is in a colour already used in the rug. Going outwards from this small border there is another band which is almost always in a pale colour and decorated with rosettes or stars enclosed in octagons. This decoration is very important because it is present in almost all Milas rugs (even in rugs with a different basic prayer-rug design) and is a distinguishing mark of carpets from this locality.

The colours of Milas prayer rugs are very beautiful and delicate. The niche is almost always in dull red with white as the ground colour of the spandrel. The predominant colours in the borders and motifs are yellow, brown and olive green as well as the same dull red used for the niche.

SIVAS
Ushak
Smyrna
Kayseri
Isparta

SIVAS

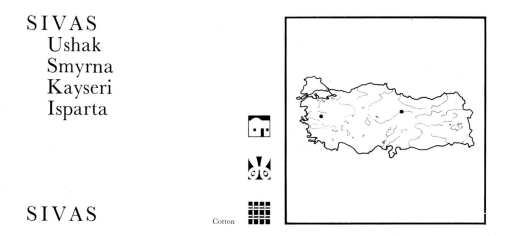

Cotton

PROVENANCE   Sivas is an important city, chief town of the region of the same name, situated in the heart of Anatolia on the banks of the Kizil Irmak river.

TECHNICAL DETAILS   Vertical loom (almost all grouped in large production centres); warp and weft in cotton, pile in wool. Turkish knot with a density of around 65 knots to the square inch. The usual sizes are 6ft 7in × 9ft 10in, and 9ft 10in × 13ft.

Ladik. The three tulip motifs which decorate the lower part of the niche are characteristic of this type of rug

100

DESCRIPTION Although they come from the heart of Anatolia, Sivas carpets bear no resemblance to the primitive nomad-type carpets woven in large numbers in this region. The Sivas motifs are clearly of Persian inspiration. The customary decoration is like that of Tabriz carpets both in the medallion and corner design and in that with a plain ground and floral and animal decorations. Up until about 1920 Sivas carpets were prized for the precision of their workmanship, the high knot density, reaching as high as 330 per square inch, and the materials used in the older carpets which were always of the highest quality. In the period between the two world wars, however, the manufacture of carpets developed apace but the quality deteriorated as a consequence.

The colours used for the ground are usually white and ivory. The designs are always in pastel shades such as pink and pistachio green. Sivas carpets can easily be distinguished from Tabriz carpets because of their less solid feel, lack of compactness in the pile in spite of close cropping, the lack-lustre quality of the wool and the use of pastel shades.

USHAK

DESCRIPTION Carpets were made at Sivas which, in technique and decoration, are typical of other carpet-making districts such as Smyrna and Ushak.

Ushak carpets, which were widely known all over Europe in the last century, have a low knot density and a deep pile. These carpets are also identifiable by the decoration, composed usually of a central medallion standing out against a plain background. The border is wide and contains few motifs and the ground is usually red. These carpets are totally unconnected with seventeenth- and eighteenth-century Ushak carpets which are very rare and costly.

Typical Milas prayer rug. The decoration and colours are characteristic of carpets from this district

SMYRNA

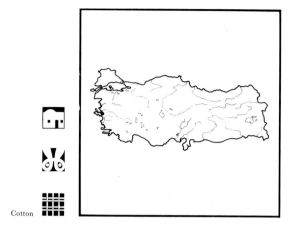

Cotton

DESCRIPTION   The carpets known as Smyrna carpets can be dealt with in conjunction with Sivas and Kayseri carpets in spite of the great distance between these different production centres. For more than a century, Smyrna (Izmir) was the centre of the Oriental carpet trade. European buyers, each with his own particular needs in mind, went to Smyrna where those needs were met by local merchants who would accept orders for any type of design at very reasonable prices.

Obviously, these were carpets woven with inferior materials and with a small number of knots to the square inch. They were made at Ushak, Isparta, and as far away as Sivas as well as at Smyrna itself.

Illustrated below are two of the guards on the border of Milas rugs. These two particular decorations facilitate the identification of carpets from this locality

KAYSERI

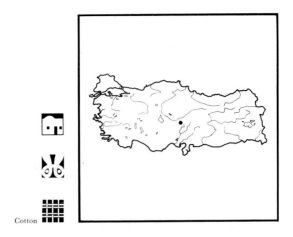

Cotton

DESCRIPTION Kayseri carpets can also be grouped with Sivas carpets because the two places are close together and the carpets have common characteristics. They are called after the town of the same name which lies about 125 miles to the south-west of Sivas. Kayseri carpets, too, have no original designs but imitate the classic motifs of Persian carpets. Their quality is generally superior to that of Sivas carpets and the pile is even more close-cropped. The field colours of Kayseri carpets may be light, or quite often dark blue or cardinal red. The colours, in fact, are often so attractive that these carpets can be forgiven their lack of originality in design.

Kayseri carpets are of both large and small dimensions and are often woven entirely in silk. (See illustration on page 95.)

ISPARTA

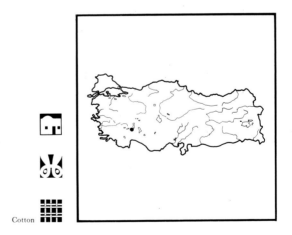

Cotton

DESCRIPTION Most of the carpets known by the name Isparta, or Sparta, were woven at Smyrna. At the beginning of the century, in fact, the well-known English firm Oriental Carpets Limited set up actual carpet-making centres at Smyrna where carpets were woven with Persian designs and techniques (Persian knot). Sparta carpets are among the best from this particular part of Turkey.

The decoration and techniques employed in Sparta carpets are very like those of the rough Tabriz carpets, but can be distinguished from them by the different feel of the fabric. They are more limp. The wool of the pile is rather lacking in lustre and the colours are usually pale with ivory predominating in the ground and pink and light blue in the decoration. (See illustration on page 96.)

A Bergama specimen from the first half of the nineteenth century. The dominant motif of the decoration is the eight-pointed star, typical of carpets from this locality and from some parts of the Caucasus. (Pars Collection, Milan)

This carpet, although of recent manufacture, keeps to the decorative motifs typical of Bergama

THE CAUCASUS

BATUM □

Derbent ●

Kuba ●

Chichi ●

Daghestan

Sumak ●

BAKU

Kazakh ●

Erivan ●

Shirvan ●

Karabagh

CHICHI

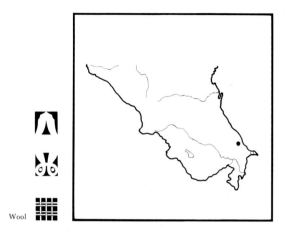

Wool

PROVENANCE   These are rugs woven by the Tchechene people who live in the south of the Caucasus.

TECHNICAL DETAILS   Horizontal loom; warp in wool; weft in either wool or cotton. The short pile is of highest quality wool. The Turkish knot is used and the density varies between 130 and 230 knots to the square inch. Chichi rugs are nearly always small, 2ft 6in–3ft 3in × 5ft–5ft 6in.

DESCRIPTION   By comparison with other Caucasian carpets, the style and motifs used in both field and border of these are immediately recognizable as being original. The border, in fact, assumes a much greater importance than the field. It is composed of a central band enclosed by a series of narrow guards on both sides. The motif used in the central band is found solely in these rugs. It is an oblong geometric figure – a kind of hexagon with four short sides – placed aslant along the border at regular intervals. The space between these figures is filled with a rosette made up of a star-like arrangement of tiny geometric shapes. The guards, on the other hand, contain motifs common to other Caucasian carpets (eight-pointed stars, triangles and diamonds with a common vertex etc.). Passing on to the field, this is decorated with lines of alternating diamonds and octagons which cover the entire area. This area, however, is often outlined by the combined triangle-diamond motif in Chichi rugs. The field diamonds are given a somewhat irregular outline by the use of a surround of hooked Greek-key motifs. The outline of the octagons is scarcely noticeable. Both shapes are decorated with eight-pointed stars or stylized floral motifs.

The complex pattern of Chichi rugs is heightened by a particularly well-balanced and pleasing colour scheme. The main background colour is yellow, while the field is nearly always a beautiful dark blue, as is also the background of the main border band. The guards, on the other hand, have a surface decoration of brown and deep red. (See illustration on page 130.)

109

Daghestan. Specimen from the first half of the nineteenth century. The field decoration is typical of the district and is particularly attractive. (Pars Collection, Milan)

DAGHESTAN

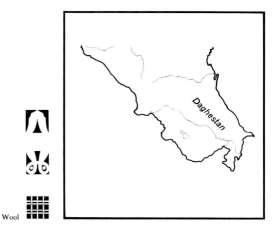

Wool

PROVENANCE   Republic of Daghestan. The country extends into the eastern part of the Caucasus up to the shores of the Caspian Sea. The principal centre is the town of Derbent where characteristic Daghestan rugs are woven (see Derbent).

TECHNICAL DETAILS   Warp and weft in wool. The warp thread, which is often quite thick and brown in colour, can easily be seen on the back of the rug. The medium deep pile is of good quality but lustreless wool. The Turkish knot is used with a density of between 53 and 100 knots per square inch. The usual dimensions are 2ft 3in × 5ft, and 3ft 3in × 9ft 10in approximately.

DESCRIPTION   Daghestan rugs are quite rare and only of old or even antique manufacture. They are almost always decorated with a special motif which facilitates identification. The field is completely divided into fairly narrow diagonal bands (2 to 4in wide) of different alternating colours. The most frequently used colours are blue in various shades, yellow, white, and a faded green.

These bands are closely decorated with small squares of different colours. At opposite corners of each square is a hooked motif. The decoration of these bands is completed by stylized roses or eight-pointed stars scattered in haphazard fashion. Another motif fairly frequently met with in Daghestan rugs is composed of three medallions of equal size covering the central part of the field. Each medallion is made up of three geometric figures. The large one is star-shaped and outlined with a line which clearly separates it from the rest of the field. Inside is another star-shaped figure but without the clearly defined outline. The latter figure in turn encloses a square decorated with simple, typically Caucasian motifs. Daghestan border patterns vary and include some of the best-known Caucasian motifs, such as the eight-pointed star and Kufic motifs. Another common border decoration is the slanting-band design similar to that used to decorate the ground of many Daghestan rugs. In fact, the border motifs are almost always on the same theme as those of the field.

112

above: *Present-day Derbent manufacture. The modern carpets from this district have a greater knot density than have the antique examples*

below: *Derbent. First half of the nineteenth century. The field decoration is of boteh motifs in one of the more formal interpretations*

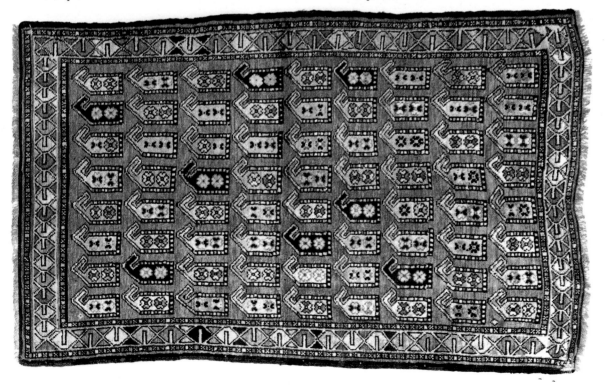

DERBENT

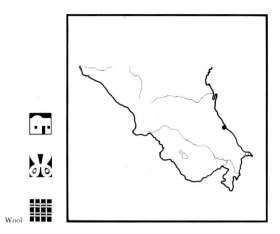

Wool

PROVENANCE   Town in Daghestan on the western shore of the Caspian Sea. Derbent is the most northerly of all the production areas of the Caucasus.

TECHNICAL DETAILS   Old or antique specimens: warp and weft in wool; often the weft is formed of two or even three threads passed between the rows of knots; rather deep pile. The knot is Turkish; the density is rather low, between 53 and 80 knots per square inch.

In recently produced carpets the backing is in cotton and the pile in close-cropped wool. The number of knots varies between 60 and 80 per square inch and they are still the Turkish type.

The usual size whatever the period of manufacture is 3ft 6in–4ft × 6ft 6in–7ft 2in. In practical terms, it is the Persian sedjadeh format with a slightly reduced width and often slightly longer by an inch or so.

DESCRIPTION   Derbent carpets, like others from the Caucasus, are not always identifiable by their design. In fact, even in this locality and especially in recent production almost all the motifs of Caucasian origin are used, and sometimes even Persian ones such as the boteh. There is, however, one motif which can be called typical of this locality, namely that made up of three medallions covering the whole of the ground. The medallions have a very clearly defined outline which sometimes resembles the Caucasian eight-pointed star and sometimes an arrow-head or a hooked Greek-key motif.

The rest of the field is decorated with Caucasian motifs, among the most common being a small medallion in the form of a stylized rose, and animal figures.

The border is quite varied, the most common being the decoration inspired by Kufic script. Other specimens have a serrated-leaf design. The colours, particularly in modern examples, are very vivid. The field is usually blue or red, and these two colours occur also in the motifs, but white, yellow and green also play an important part.

opposite page, above:
Karabagh. The field motif of this example clearly shows the influence of Savonnerie decoration

opposite page, below: *Karabagh carpet decorated with the herati field motif*

114

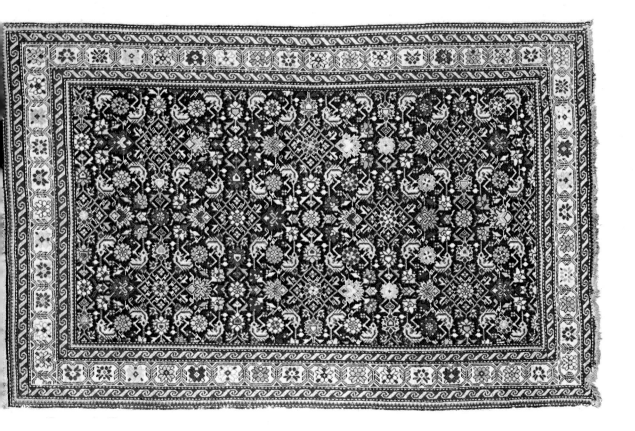

KARABAGH

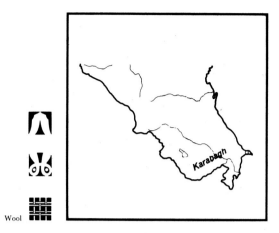

Wool

PROVENANCE   Southern region of the Caucasus on the borders of Persia. This part of the Caucasus is inhabited by mainly Armenian people. Karabagh carpets are woven all over the region, particularly in the centre of Shusha.

TECHNICAL DETAILS   Karabagh carpets are all in wool – warp, weft and pile. The depth of the pile varies according to the design and the place of origin. It is deep in the examples with French-type motifs (Savonnerie) and short in specimens with noticeably angular motifs of Persian origin (diamond-shaped medallions on a self-colour field like those in the antique carpets from Khorassan and Ferahan). The Turkish knot is used in the Karabagh with a density which varies between 60 and 160 knots per square inch. Karabagh carpets vary considerably in size. The most common forms are the sedjadeh which is, however, larger than the Persian ones (5ft 3in × 7ft 3in) and the kelleys (5ft–6ft 6in × 13ft–16ft 6in).

DESCRIPTION   Karabagh carpets, in spite of their lack of originality in design (mostly Persian and Western), reveal straight away their high stylistic level.

In this region, in fact, the history of the carpet is lost in antiquity. Very probably, the majority of antique carpets which are known as Armenian dragon carpets or simply as Caucasian, originated in Karabagh. As has already been mentioned, a variety of motifs both geometric and floral are used in these carpets. The most common decorative motifs are:

HERATI DESIGN   This is the same design as can be found in carpets from so many Persian sources, particularly those from Senneh and Ferahan, but in Karabagh carpets the herati design is used on a larger scale. Very often the border of these carpets bears a floral motif taken from Western-style Karabagh which helps in the identification of these herati Karabagh carpets.

The colours, too, are typical of this region: the ground colours being dark – red, dark blue and black – and the motifs being in rather vivid colours – yellow, pink, light green and bright red.

116

MEDALLION DESIGN   These are exclusively stair carpets and kelleys where the ground is self-colour and is decorated with medallions in the Khorassan style (tending towards floral), or Ferahan style (with a medallion shaped like an elongated diamond).

In these carpets also the colours are typical (dark ground with brightly coloured motifs).

BOTEH DESIGN   The boteh motif, typical of many parts of Persia, is used also in Karabagh carpets. The stylized approach and the arrangement of the boteh in diagonal lines with the points turned alternately left and right are reminiscent of the Seraband use of the boteh.

SAVONNERIE FLORAL DESIGN   As early as the eighteenth century some Karabagh carpets were woven where the motif used for decoration was a floral one clearly inspired by Savonnerie work. In this period, Savonnerie carpets had achieved world fame and many examples had arrived in the East, brought back by dignitaries and merchants returning from their travels in Europe. Naturally, Caucasian craftsmen were not up to using the techniques employed for a completely floral design. They were only accustomed to making designs in straight lines or angles of forty-five degrees. But the beauty of the Savonnerie-inspired Karabagh carpets lies in just that primitive technique of execution allied to an instinctive sense of proportion and an exquisite blend of colours.

According to the degree of stylization to which the original motif was subjected, these carpets have either a field completely decorated by a repeated motif very similar to Savonnerie patterns, or flower posies repeated a few times and thrown into prominence by the dark colour of the background.

In spite of the variety of their designs, Karabagh carpets are easily recognizable because of the uniformity of the colours, the materials used, and the employment of the Turkish knot.

Whether their motifs are of Persian or French origin, however, these carpets are of a rare beauty and fascinate the carpet enthusiast.

above: *A splendid Kazakh specimen. The use of the eight-pointed star may be noted in the border decoration*
opposite page:
Characteristic Kazakh adler motif

KAZAKH

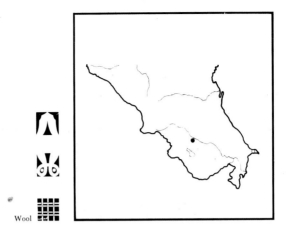

Wool

PROVENANCE   Kazakh carpets are woven by semi-nomadic shepherds living in the mountainous region in the heart of the Caucasus. They are called after the town of the same name which is the main centre of the region.

TECHNICAL DETAILS   Warp and weft in wool; the weft threads are always red or brown and three are woven in between the rows of knots; the weft is therefore easily visible on the back of the carpet; the wool pile is fairly deep.

The yarn used is always of excellent quality and gives the carpet a lustrous appearance and a wearing quality which has become a byword.

The Turkish knot is used and the density varies between 53 and 100 knots to the square inch. Kazakh carpets are made in a number of sizes. The most usual is 5ft–5ft 6in × 7ft–8ft. Small Kazakhs (2ft 3in–3ft × 4ft 6in–5ft 6in) and long ones (kelleys) are also quite common.

DESCRIPTION   The principal characteristic of Kazakh carpets is the linear nature of the design. In no other area, in fact, are carpets woven with such a formal decoration. Kazakh carpets are also recognizable by some typical motifs which we shall now describe.

opposite page, above left:
*Small Kazakh specimen decorated
with octagonal-shaped and
rhombus motifs*

above right: *Kazakh. The
beauty of this specimen is due to
the combination of colours, which
are unusual but which harmonize
well with one another*

below: *Typical Kazakh runner.
Note the running-dog motif which
surrounds each of the four
octagons of the field decoration*

KAZAKH ADLER

DESCRIPTION   These carpets are among the most highly esteemed carpets from this locality. The name adler, eagle in German, became associated with these carpets because of the similarity of their principal motif to the eagle of a coat-of-arms. The adler motif takes up almost the entire width of the field. It is repeated several times along the length and thus covers almost the whole of it. In some examples the last motif is cut off halfway by the border, which confirms that these carpets were of primitive and nomadic manufacture.

The adler design consists of a cross with two arms of equal length ending in a point. This is always in a dark colour and is decorated with geometric plant motifs such as tulips and roses and outlined by a long irregular motif on a white background which resembles the wing opening of an eagle. The rest of the field of these carpets is entirely decorated with typical Caucasian ornamentation: lozenges, stars, rosettes and stylized human and animal figures.

The designs are executed in an extremely formal manner and follow no pre-ordained decorative composition.

CENTRAL MEDALLION KAZAKH

DESCRIPTION   This particular type of central medallion Kazakh carpet has a single large central octagonal medallion. Inside the octagon, usually on a white background, there is another geometric figure, usually a square. The central medallion itself is also enclosed in a square.

The rest of the ground is also decorated with geometric figures, mostly squares and rectangles. The small motifs are almost always made up of eight-pointed stars, rosettes, and stylized animals.

REPEATED DESIGN KAZAKH

DESCRIPTION   The field of these repeated design Kazakh carpets is decorated by a succession of octagons about eight inches in size of different colours. Inside the octagons there are various geometric shapes, often ending in a hooked Greek key. This decoration is especially to be found in small Kazakh carpets and in the long ones.

MULTIPLE MEDALLION KAZAKH

DESCRIPTION   This is the Kazakh design which is closest to certain Persian styles such as Ferahan.

The ground decoration is a succession of diamond-shaped medallions decorated with the same motif in different colours. It is a typical motif of the long Kazakh carpets (5ft 6in × 13ft approximately).

BORDERS   All these different patterns have border and colour range in common. The typically Caucasian borders are of limited size and are made up for the most part of a large central band and two narrower guards. The central band is decorated with either a serrated-leaf motif or alternating eight-pointed stars and rosettes.

Sometimes the border decoration is reduced to simple geometric motifs. In some examples the outer guard is decorated with the hooked motif called running dog.

above: *Rare nineteenth-century Shirvan specimen. This is a carpet of particularly fine workmanship*

below: *Shirvan runner. Note the original motif in the central band of the border*

The dyes used are quite vivid but are combined with a good sense of colour and create a very fine effect. The most common colours are red and blue for the field with motifs in white, yellow, green and light blue.

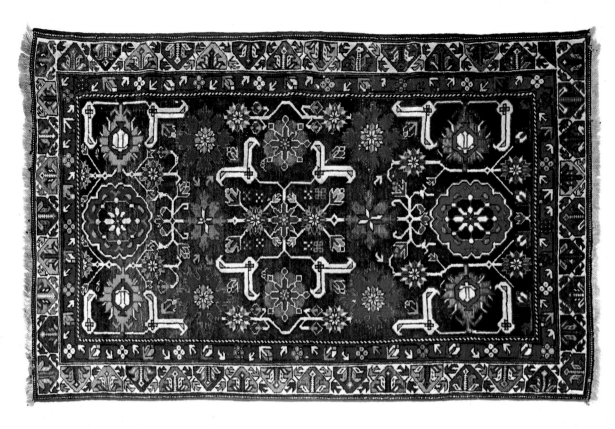

opposite page, above: *Shirvan.*
The field decoration has a Persian-
inspired motif: the harshang or
crab.

Opposite page below:
Nineteenth-century Shirvan.
The wider band of the border
is of particular interest. This
is known as a Kufic border
because it is inspired by the script
of that name

below: *A magnificent example of*
a Shirvan from the first half of the
nineteenth century. Note the
pleasing combination of colours
and the accurate detail of the work

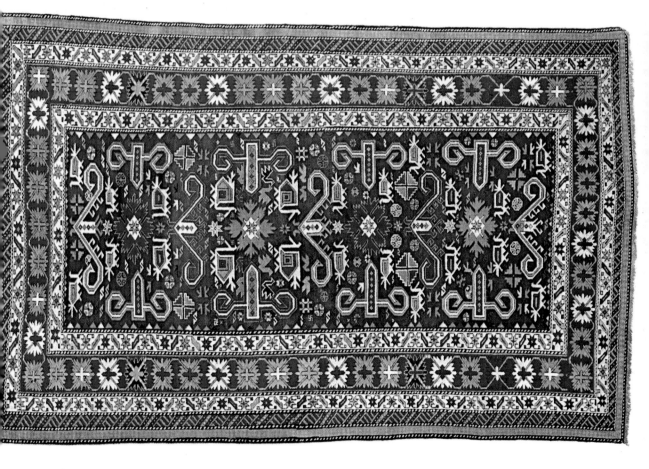

SHIRVAN

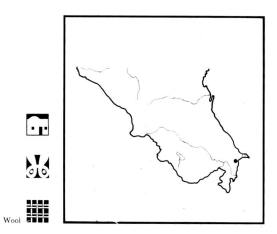

Wool

PROVENANCE   The village of Shirvan is situated near the south-west shore of the Caspian Sea and the district of the same name in the southern part of Azerbaijan.

TECHNICAL DETAILS   The warp and weft is in wool in the antique specimens, in wool or cotton in those woven between 1850 and 1920, and completely in cotton in modern examples.

The pile is always in close-cropped wool. Some late eighteenth- and early nineteenth-century examples have a rather deeper pile.

The Turkish knot is used with a density of 100 to 200 knots to the square inch. The modern carpets usually have a higher knot density than the older or antique ones.

Shirvan carpets are woven in various sizes but are most commonly in the small or long narrow shapes.

DESCRIPTION   As with other Caucasian carpets, Shirvans have a widely varied decoration. It must be remembered that this region was subjected to a number of invasions, hence the variety of motifs used in the decoration of the carpet.

In the Safavid period (sixteenth century) the craft of carpet-making flourished in this area. It is therefore understandable that Persian influence may be seen in Shirvan carpets, for example, in the use of the harshang or crab design. This is clearly a design which was originally floral although in Shirvan carpets it becomes rather formalized. It probably dates from the Shah Abbas period (1587–1629).

The harshang motif is composed of large flowers in a combination which resembles a crab in shape.

The field is completely covered with lines of these flowers in different sizes (see illustration on page 123).

The decoration of this type of Shirvan carpet is often completed by a border of Caucasian origin known as a Kufic border because it resembles Kufic characters.

Another recurrent theme in Shirvan carpets consists of a field decoration of stylized flowers and animal figures. In the centre of the field is a line of eight-

126

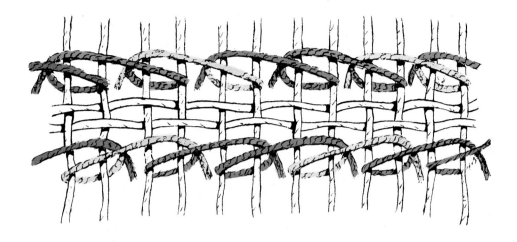

Technique for Sumak work. The coloured threads are those which show when the work is finished

pointed stars, rosettes and various geometric motifs. The border often contains serrated leaves. This type of decoration is particularly prevalent in the long narrow rugs.

The small Shirvan rugs can be both in prayer rug or in normal form. In both cases the decoration is made up for the most part of a design composed of minute stylized diamonds and tulips or boteh motifs. Shirvan rugs are very varied in colour. Usually the ground is in some sober colour such as dark blue, while the motifs are quite vivid. White is predominant in the border.

SUMAK

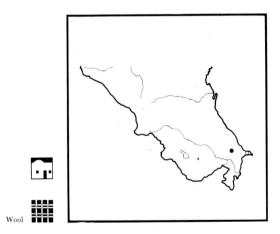

Wool

PROVENANCE   The carpet-making centre of Sumak lies about thirty miles from Baku, a major Russian port on the Caspian Sea.

These carpets are woven not only in Sumak itself but also in the vast area which includes southern Daghestan and Azerbaijan.

127

above left: *Typical Sumak carpet in terms of both colour and decoration. This example is from the nineteenth century.*

above right: *Verne specimen from the nineteenth century. Its beauty lies in its harmony of colour and simplicity of design*

128

TECHNICAL DETAILS   The main characteristic of Sumak carpets is that, unlike most Oriental carpets, they have no knotted pile. They are weft-face carpets, that is, the weft is visible and forms the pile. Nowadays this type of technique is restricted to Sumak and the neighbouring centres of Sile and Verne, while a similar weft-face technique has given its name to the kilims of Senneh and some areas inhabited by the nomads of Anatolia. Formerly this type of technique was used in many different places.

Probably one of the best-known carpets of this genre is the famous Spring-time of Chosroes (see page 18). Similar carpets are made at Kashan. Sumak carpets are composed solely of warp and weft threads. Both are almost exclusively in wool except for a few rare specimens of little value which have a cotton warp. The weft is made up of two different threads; the first constitutes the decoration of the carpet while the second, as in the normal type of carpet, is used to strengthen the fabric.

The thread used for decoration is wrapped around the warp threads to form a kind of chain stitch which is raised above the normal weft (see sketch on page 127). The decorative weft thread is not as long as the width of the carpet but is changed every time a new colour is needed. A longish piece of thread is left at each end and is visible on the reverse of the carpet. These specimens are woven in various sizes which range from very tiny ones used as pouches by the nomads to carpets measuring 11ft 6in × 8ft 3in. The most common measurement lies between 5ft–6ft 7in × 8ft 3in–9ft 10in.

In spite of the lack of pile, Sumak carpets are very strong, thanks to the quality of material used and to the double weft which makes the fabric compact. It is, however, necessary to take great care of Sumak carpets and to use an underfelt to make them lie securely on the floor.

DESCRIPTION   Quite apart from the technique of Sumak carpets, their markedly geometric decoration makes them easily recognizable.

In the border, as well as the usual bands one wide and two narrow there is a fourth band outside decorated with a hooked Greek-key motif.

The two guards and sometimes also the main band are decorated with the eight-pointed star or a rosette in a diamond. Generally, the field decoration is of three or four motifs in the shape of diamonds or rectangles and diamonds one above the other.

These large geometric forms are in dark blue in contrast with the rest of the field which is usually in dull red. In the field between one diamond and another there are very often large octagons in fairly bright colours, often yellow or green. The whole carpet is closely decorated with geometric motifs, almost all those met with in Caucasian carpets.

Sumak carpets are undoubtedly the most beautiful Caucasian carpets as much for their rich but extremely geometric decoration as for the very lively and well-blended colours.

*Chichi. A rare and magnificent
specimen from the beginning of the
nineteenth century. In spite of the
abundance of decorative motifs the
carpet is extremely pleasing.
(Private Collection, Milan)*

IRAN

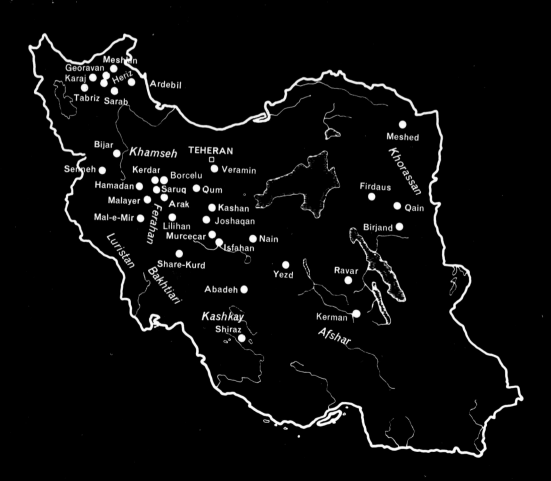

Meshkin
Georavan
Karaj ● ● ● Heriz
Tabriz Sarab
Ardebil

Meshed

Bijar
Senneh ● *Khamseh*   TEHERAN
□
Kerdar
Borcelu ● Veramin
Hamadan ● ● Saruq ● Qum
Malayer ● Arak
Mal-e-Mir ● ● Kashan
Lilihan ● Joshaqan
Murcecar ● ● Nain
● Isfahan

Ferahan

Khorassan

Firdaus
● Qain

Birjand ●

Luristan

Bakhtiari

Share-Kurd
Yezd
Ravar

Abadeh ●

Kashkay
Shiraz
Kerman
Afshar

ABADEH

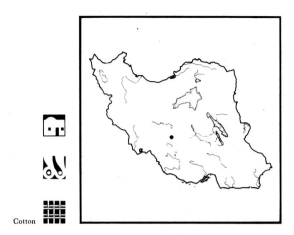

Cotton

PROVENANCE   A village about 125 miles to the south of Isfahan along the Isfahan-Shiraz road. To the west of Abadeh is the tableland inhabited by the Fars.

TECHNICAL DETAILS   Vertical loom; warp and weft of cotton, wool pile. The knotting is by no means the finest to be found, but is very regular. The Persian knot is used and the density varies between 130 and 200 knots to the square inch. The usual sizes are 6ft 6in–8ft × 9ft 10in–11ft, and the sedjadeh type (4ft–4ft 6in × 6ft 6in–7ft 3in).

DESCRIPTION   All Abedeh carpets are of recent manufacture, the carpet-making craft in this district dating back only a few decades.

The designs used, therefore, are not those handed down from generation to generation and linked to local tradition, but are taken from carpets from other parts of Iran.

The classic Persian zil-i-soltan motif, which takes the form of a vase of roses usually repeated so as to cover the field completely, is the commonest motif of Abadeh carpets. Because the knot used in this district is somewhat large, however, the motif loses some of its original harmony and studied refinement. In any case, in Abadeh carpets, the zil-i-soltan motif is reproduced in a rather larger size than is usual. Another decoration frequently found in Abadeh carpets derives from designs used by the Kashkay tribe for their own carpets. This tribe sets up its tents near Abadeh during the summer months.

In this type of Abadeh a single diamond shape, which is the principal decorative motif of Kashkay carpets, is used in the centre of the field. All the rest of the carpet is decorated with small geometric designs. These are similar to the motifs used by the Fars tribe.

Abadeh borders are small by comparison with the field and they are usually formed by two guards framing a main central band which stands out by virtue of its different background colour. The colours used are vivid: flame and cobalt blue. Although these carpets have no roots in ancient tradition, they are to be recommended because of the pleasing simplicity of their decoration and for their great wearing qualities.

132

*Abadeh specimen of modern
manufacture decorated with the
zil-i-soltan motif*

AFSHAR

Cotton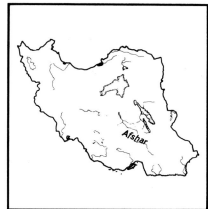
Wool

PROVENANCE   These are rugs which come from the nomadic Afshar tribe who live on the tableland to the south of Kerman and from the villages in the surrounding area.

TECHNICAL DETAILS   Rugs woven by the nomads; ground loom; wool or cotton warp; wool weft with a single thread between the rows of knots. The pile is wool and there are between 40 and 105 Turkish knots to the square inch.

For rugs woven in the villages the loom is vertical. Both warp and weft are always in cotton, the knot is Persian, and the density between 40 and 100 knots to the square inch.

The customary shapes are the zaronim (3ft 6in × 5ft) and the dozar (4ft 6in × 7ft). Large carpets are rare.

DESCRIPTION   The Afshar tribe originated in Azerbaijan, a region to the north of Iran inhabited by Turks. During the reign of Shah Tahmasp (1524–1587) the Afshar tribe was driven southwards into the zone it now occupies because of the stormy character of its members. As the centuries passed, the Afshar rugs came under the influence of designs used by the craftsmen of Kerman and by the neighbouring Fars tribe, and for this reason the decoration of Afshar rugs is very varied. The most common types are:

AFSHAR DEHAJ   The decoration of these rugs consists of large geometric boteh motifs. These boteh cover the whole field of the rug.

AFSHAR MORGI   Morgi in Persian means chicken. These Afshar rugs are, in fact, decorated by a repeating geometric motif resembling a chicken which covers the whole field of the rug. This is far and away the most original and interesting Afshar decoration.

DIAMOND AFSHAR   These are rugs decorated with motifs taken from those used for Shiraz carpets. Usually there are two diamonds, or, more rarely, one or three. The whole field is tightly packed with small designs which often reveal the floral influence of nearby Kerman.

FLORAL AFSHAR   These specimens are woven in villages near Kerman and the designs are inspired by the carpets from that town. The decoration is therefore floral, almost always in repeating motifs, rarely with a central medallion.

The most commonly found ground colours are ivory and bright red. These two colours also occur in the designs along with light and dark blue and yellow.

As is often the case in Persian carpets, the borders are limited in proportion to the whole carpet. They are classic borders with a central band and two flanking guards. The serrated-leaf border is quite common in Afshar Dehaj rugs. This demonstrates once again the northerly origin of the Afshar tribe. The other motifs often include a decoration formed by a succession of diamond shapes in different sizes.

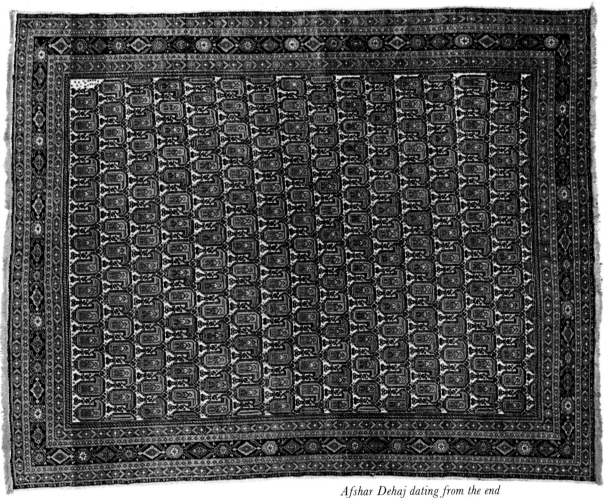

Afshar Dehaj dating from the end of the nineteenth century. The motif of the field decoration is boteh

ARDEBIL
Sarab
Meshkin

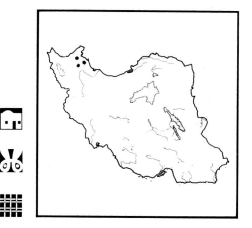

ARDEBIL

Cotton

Wool

PROVENANCE   Ardebil is an Iranian village on the border with the Caucasus situated in the mountains of Azerbaijan overlooking the Caspian Sea.

TECHNICAL DETAILS   Vertical loom; warp and weft usually in cotton, sometimes in wool. The woollen pile is of medium depth, the Turkish knot is used with a density varying between 60 and 120 knots to the square inch. The most commonly found dimensions are approximately 4ft 6in × 7ft and 5ft × 7ft 6in.

DESCRIPTION   The name Ardebil is associated with the very beautiful sixteenth-century specimens such as the one exhibited at the Victoria and Albert Museum in London. These were the first of the floral-type carpets made to the order of the Safavid court during the reign of Shah Tahmasp. Recent Ardebil carpets have nothing in common with these antique specimens. They are carpets with geometric motifs clearly inspired by Caucasian designs. In particular, they resemble Shirvan carpets but differ from them in three aspects.

The first is the different decoration of the border: in Ardebil carpets the border is much more elaborate and is often made up of a central band framed by a series of guards. These guards are decorated with rosettes and octagonal stars as well as with a series of other geometric shapes which, in Shirvan carpets, usually decorate the whole field.

The second factor is the quality of the wool. The wool used for the pile of Ardebil carpets is lustreless and the yarn is rather thick. Also the depth of the pile is greater than in Shirvan carpets.

The third element is the colour scheme. The field of Ardebil carpets is usually ivory and the dyes used for the motifs are very vivid, with wide use of red and pea green.

The commonest ground decoration in Ardebil carpets is made up of three diamonds in line in the centre of the carpet, often outlined with a Greek-key motif. The rest of the field is completely covered with very varied Caucasian motifs: rosettes, stars, animal and human figures and geometric shapes.

136

Late nineteenth-century Meshkin stair carpet. The wool used for the field retains its natural colour

Modern Ardebil carpet

SARAB

DESCRIPTION   About eighteen miles to the west of Ardebil is the village of Sarab, famed for the production of stair carpets. Here, too, the designs are geometric and of Caucasian influence. The most frequently found decoration is made up of diamond shapes on a self-colour background, usually natural camel colour. A characteristic of the Sarab border is in the outside part which is often finished off with a strip of self-colour weave of the same colour as the field. Sarab carpets are very attractive and of extremely high quality.

MESHKIN

DESCRIPTION   Meshkin carpets have similar characteristics to those from Sarab and are woven in the village of the same name which lies on the Caucasian frontier. Meshkin carpets always have a wool warp and weft and the decoration is clearly Caucasian. They are much prized for the soft velvety quality of the wool.

138

BAKHTIARI

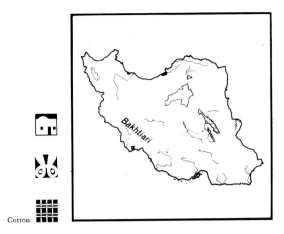

Cotton

PROVENANCE   Carpets from the Chahar Mahal region in central Iran and bounded to the west and south by the Sagros mountains and to the north by the Zaindeh river which flows through Isfahan.

TECHNICAL DETAILS   Loom is almost always vertical, but in the most isolated villages the nomad-type ground loom is still used. Warp and weft usually in cotton but sometimes in wool. The weft is composed of two threads. The wool pile is of medium depth and the knot is nearly always Turkish, but the Persian knot is used for carpets made in the village of Shahr Kord. The number of knots varies from 80 to 120 to the square inch. The finest quality, which has a single weft thread and exceeds 120 knots per square inch, is called bibibaff. Bakhtiari carpets are made in various sizes, sometimes very large.

The usual shapes are the sedjadeh and kelley, the latter in a small size 5ft–5ft 6in × 8ft 10in–10ft 6in. The long shapes are prevalent among old Bakhtiari carpets.

DESCRIPTION   Bakhtiari carpets are easily identifiable because of their special designs. The field on the carpet is almost always divided into squares or diamonds made to stand out by a plain outline. These geometric figures are decorated either with animal or plant motifs, particularly cypresses and flowering shrubs. Each carpet may contain more than ten different designs. Another fairly common decoration is a formal repeated design of flowers and shrubs which covers the whole field. Often these specimens contain a tree of life in the central part of the field.

Some Bakhtiari carpets are made by the craftsmen in the village of Shahr Kord. These carpets are made by Bakhtiari tribesmen who have given up their nomadic life, and reveal the influence of nearby Isfahan in the techniques employed, the use of the Persian knot and the decoration. The design is floral with a central medallion. The execution of this design is, however, more formal and betrays the nomadic origin of the craftsmen.

The border is typical of many Persian carpets from different regions: two narrow guards and a wide central band. The decorative motifs are very varied. The herati border motif is usually used for carpets woven in Shahr Kord. In the nomad carpets, particularly the older and antique ones, the border is often decorated with a serrated-leaf pattern. Another fairly common border is one where the decoration is a succession of cartouches in which the principal motifs of the ground decoration appear on a white background. All Bakhtiari carpets are in dark colours, deep red, yellow ochre, bottle green, dark brown and bright blue.

Many carpets from this region are also known by the name of their village of origin. This is the case with Heinegun carpets which have similar characteristics to those from Bakhtiari.

opposite page, above: *Typical late nineteenth-century Bakhtiari carpet. The field decoration includes a line of octagons which contain stylized plant motifs. Although many different ground colours are used, the overall effect is pleasing*

below: *Bakhtiari specimen made in Shahr Kord. The decoration of this carpet is clearly inspired by flowers, while the central medallion and corners show the influence of Isfahan motifs*

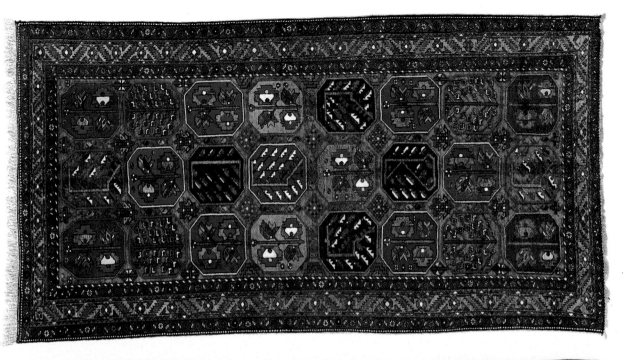
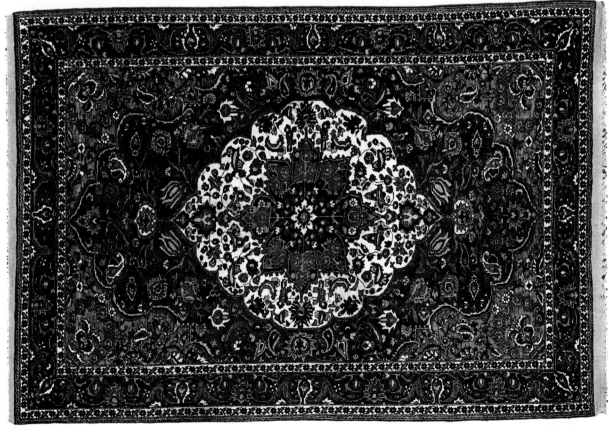

BIJAR

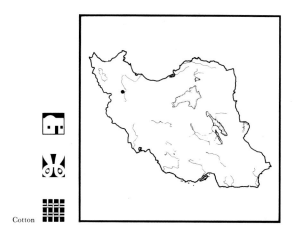

Cotton

PROVENANCE   Small agricultural town in Kurdistan lying some thirty miles from the main town of Senneh. Bijar suffered great damage during two world wars and a famine in 1918–1919 decimated its population.

TECHNICAL DETAILS   Very rudimentary vertical loom. The warp is in cotton or, more rarely, in wool. The weft is formed by thin wool threads and thick cotton ones. The close-cut pile is of high quality lustrous wool. The knot is Turkish and the density varies between 100 and 210 knots to the square inch. The weft is usually of as many as five threads, four loose wool ones and one taut cotton one in the centre. This is the chief characteristic of Bijar carpets. These warp threads are beaten in with two kinds of tool – the usual comb beater, and a special one which resembles an enormous iron claw. The weaver inserts the claw between the warp threads and beats in the weft threads many times. This special technique makes Bijar carpets very compact and heavy. They must never be folded with the pile inwards because the warp and weft is so tight that it would break. All the characteristic Persian shapes are used and the most common sizes are 4ft–4ft 3in × 6ft 6in–7ft 3in and 6ft 6in–8ft × 9ft 10in–11ft.

DECORATION   Bijar carpets, like those from Saruq, are often decorated with floral motifs in a formal interpretation which betrays their primitive style. The result is a less sophisticated decoration than that from classic Persian sources but decidedly more restrained and attractive. There is often a medallion in the centre of the carpet, while the rest of the field is decorated either with floral designs or with the herati motif reproduced in a small size and repeated to cover the whole background.

The herati design is also the most common decoration in Bijar carpets with a self-colour field.

Other examples have only a central medallion standing out against a self-colour field. In these carpets the four quarters have a floral ornamentation.

Bijar borders are often composed of five bands, four narrow and one central wide one. The main band is often decorated with border boteh, while the guards contain a succession of rosettes alternating with stylized flower motifs. Another fairly common border is made up of two very narrow guards and a central one

142

Magnificent nineteenth-century Bijar specimen. The field decoration is lively and pleasing. The almost black background makes the motifs appear to stand out in relief. (Private Collection, Milan)

*Nineteenth-century Bijar
decorated with herati motifs*

which, although wider than the guards, is small in relation to the size of the carpet. In this type of border, a rich floral decoration is often added to the border herati.

Bijar carpets are identifiable not only by their unusual technique but also by their very beautiful colours. The ground shades are dark: dark blue, cherry red and bottle green are common, while the colours used for the designs are very vivid and often include a delightful turquoise. Bijar carpets are proverbially sturdy and beautifully coloured, and because production has been limited for more than twenty years, they are very rare.

144

FERAHAN
MALAYER

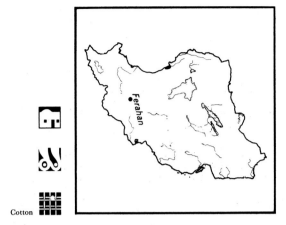

Cotton

PROVENANCE   Ferahan is the district of Iran situated between the towns of Arak and Saruq. Ferahan carpets were woven in the city of Mushkabad which was destroyed in the last century by Fath Ali Shah. Except for a few rare examples coming from the village of Ibrahimabad, they are no longer made.

TECHNICAL DETAILS   Vertical loom; warp and weft in cotton. The weft is formed by a double thread of very thick strong cotton which is easily visible on the reverse of the carpet. The pile is in a very close-cropped wool. The knot is almost always Persian with a density varying from 80 to 160 knots to the square inch. Although the fabric is very fine, Ferahan carpets are very strong. The most common shape is the kelley from 5ft × 10ft to 8ft 3in × 20ft.

DESCRIPTION   The decoration of Ferahan carpets has also been influenced by the herati motif. In many examples the whole of the field of the carpet is completely decorated with them. In other Ferahans the centre of the carpet has one or two elongated diamond-shaped medallions. These medallions, which are always decorated with the herati motif, stand out from the rest of the field because of the different colour of the background (dark blue or cherry red for the field, and white or dark blue for the medallion).

The border is very important in the decoration of Ferahan carpets. It is usually made up of a succession of narrow and closely-decorated bands. The outer bands have distinctly geometric designs, while the internal ones have stylized flowers and often the boteh motif. The principal band is mostly decorated with border herati. Some very fine and rare Ferahan carpets have the zil-i-soltan motif in both field and border.

The predominant colours of Ferahan carpets are various shades of red and dark blue for the field. In the border these two dominant colours are repeated and other vivid colours are added such as yellow, light green, azure and white.

Carpets with similar characteristics to the Ferahan carpets are the old Malayer carpets, woven in the city of the same name situated to the west of the district of Ferahan. Ferahan and Malayer carpets are restrained and of very high class. They are very much prized in England and were frequently to be found in the great houses of the Victorian period.

145

opposite page: *Rare early nineteenth-century Ferahan specimen. The border and field are decorated with the zil-i-soltan motif. A Greek-key design made up of a succession of tiny boteh motifs runs around the field. (Pars Collection, Milan)*

this page: *Nineteenth-century Ferahan specimen. There is an unusual contrast between the very rich border decoration and the self-colour field. (Private Collection, Milan)*

following page: *Nineteenth-century Malayer. The field and corner decorations contain the classic herati motif*

HAMADAN
Mazlaghan
Mahal
Lilihan
Mushkabad

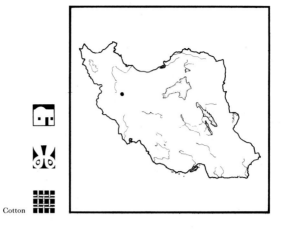

Cotton

HAMADAN

PROVENANCE   Hamadan rises above the Iranian tableland at some 7,000 feet above sea level near to the ruins of ancient Ecbatana. Hamadan and the villages of the province are the most important centres of carpet production in Iran.

TECHNICAL DETAILS   Vertical loom; warp and weft in cotton. Usually the weft is a single thread. Pile in wool; Turkish knot with a density varying between 30 and 100 knots to the square inch. Almost all Hamadan carpets have a fringe on one side while the opposite side terminates in a narrow selvedge. The usual dimensions are the dozar (4ft–4ft 6in × 6ft–6ft 6in) and the stair-carpet or strip (kenareh) measuring 2ft 3in–4ft × 8ft 3in–20ft.

DESCRIPTION   The majority of carpets known as Hamadan come from around fifty villages scattered over an area some sixty miles around the city. At Hamadan there are some craft centres which were created at the beginning of this century. On the whole, Hamadan production is rather mundane so far as decoration and weave is concerned. The materials, by contrast, are of a very good quality. The different Hamadan areas are often called, improperly, Mosul, perhaps because it was to this city that carpets made in western Persia were sent for onward transmission to Constantinople. The best-known carpets of the Hamadan group are Borchelu and Khamseh. The first are carpets woven in the villages found to the east of Hamadan. The field is usually decorated with herati motifs on a red background. Often, too, there is a central medallion, sometimes floral and sometimes geometric, on an ivory background. The four corners repeat the central medallion pattern.

The border is the classic one of three bands; the two guards have rosettes joined by a snake-like decoration and the central one repeats the decorative motifs of the field.

Khamseh is a region situated to the north of Hamadan. Khamseh carpets are among the best of the region. Their decoration has a central medallion in geometric form.

These examples have four quarters at the sides which are triangular and are decorated with the same motifs as the central medallion. The border is formed by three bands with various decorations and very stylized designs.

149

MAZLAGHAN

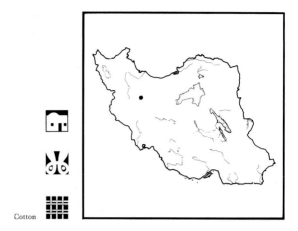

DESCRIPTION   Carpets known by this name come from the village of Kerdar situated to the north-east of Hamadan. The field in these carpets has a pair of zig-zag lines along its length which resemble a thunderbolt. Within this motif there is a central medallion, while the four quarters are closely decorated with rosettes and stars.

The border is the usual three-band type. The two guards have a decoration formed by rosettes and a snake-like pattern, while the central band may vary. Some have a serrated-leaf design; some repeat the rosettes from the corners, while others have an original design vaguely reminiscent of a crab.

The predominant colours are red and blue; also camel wool in its natural colour is used to quite a large extent.

MAHAL

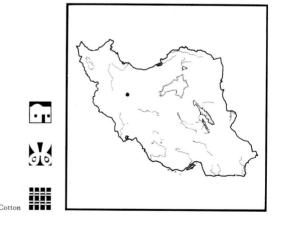

DESCRIPTION   In spite of the fact that these carpets come from the town of Arak and its environs, as do the two following ones, Lilihan and Mushkabad, they are considered as belonging to the Hamadan family. Mahal carpets are easily recognizable because of their large knots and their softness. The decoration is either floral, but with large simple motifs, or of geometric style with a central diamond. The border is extremely simple and is of the traditional three-band type.

LILIHAN

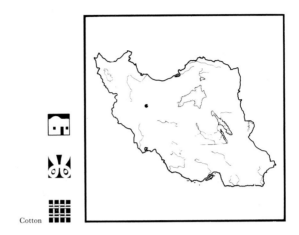

DESCRIPTION   Carpets woven in a group of villages inhabited by Armenians. The Lilihan carpets are recognizable for their beautiful colours, particularly blue and azure in all the various shades. The design is floral but with large and stylized motifs. Often Lilihan carpets are produced in the small form of the kelley (6ft × 12ft). The decorative composition of the border is quite varied and repeats the floral motifs of the field.

MUSHKABAD

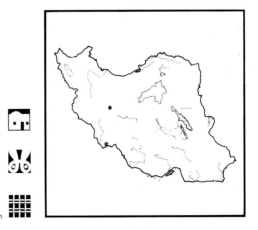

DESCRIPTION · These carpets, too, are woven in the region around Arak. They have a very even weave, a deep pile and a floral design which is rich in motifs and colours. The border is the traditional three-band type decorated with floral designs repeating those of the field, or with the herati border motif.

151

above: *Mazlaghan. These carpets come from the village of Kerdar, situated in the agricultural region of Hamadan. They are easily recognizable because of the arrow motifs which outline the central part of the field*

opposite page, above: *Typical Hamadan specimen. A characteristic of these carpets is the central medallion which uses the same colours as the four corners*

below: *Khamseh. Characteristic carpet from this locality. Note the natural wool colour of the ground*

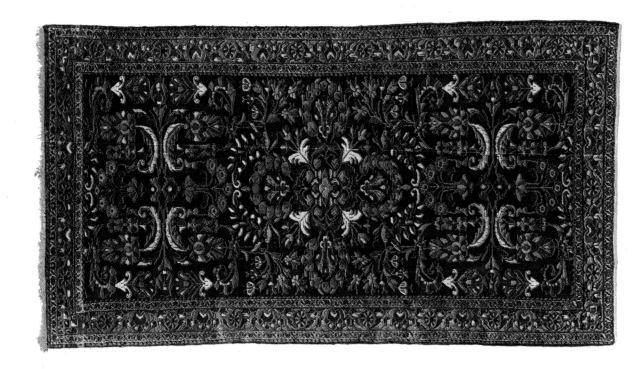

above: *Lilihan. This specimen and the one shown below come from a district to the south of the Hamadan region. Note the field decoration which is a geometric interpretation of a floral design*

left: *Mushkabad. The field of this carpet is decorated with a niche motif. Note the two columns formed by flower motifs one above the other*

ISFAHAN

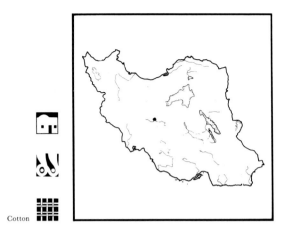

Cotton

PROVENANCE   Isfahan carpets are woven in the city of the same name and in the neighbouring villages. Isfahan, which was the capital of Persia during the reign of Shah Abbas, preserves in its monuments the pomp and art of the Persian renaissance. Situated in the centre of Iran in the fertile plain of the Zaiandeh river, it is one of the most prestigious cities of the Middle East. Its Shah and Lutfullah mosques are famous. It was in the reign of the Safavid ruler, Ali Kapu, that these were erected on an enormous square where, in the time of Shah Abbas, polo games took place, polo being the Persian national sport.

TECHNICAL DETAILS   Vertical loom, mostly in private houses in the poor quarters of the city. Backing in cotton; pile in very close cropped wool, some examples having a silk pile.

The Persian knot is used and the density is very high: from 160 to 400 knots per square inch, and silk carpets have a knot density approaching 600 to the square inch. The usual measurements are 4ft–4ft 6in × 6ft 3in–7ft 3in, 6ft 6in–7ft 3in × 9ft 10in–10ft 10in.

DESCRIPTION   Isfahan carpets were probably the first Persian carpets to be known and appreciated in Europe. In fact, during the reign of Shah Abbas (1587–1629) many carpets woven by the craftsmen of Isfahan were given as gifts to dignitaries and rulers from the West. These examples were in silk and sometimes included the use of silver and gold thread. However, after the city was occupied by the Afghans, carpet-making was practically abandoned. Once the support of the court was gone, the artisans of Isfahan, who were famous for their skill, preferred to dedicate themselves to activities which offered them a much more rapid chance of making money, such as miniatures, engraving in silver and copper, and the weaving of costly materials. It was only at the beginning of this century that carpet-making was taken up again, and in a few years it regained all its old fame. The credit for this is due to the fine ustad who created most beautiful cartoons, using the antique designs.

Isfahan carpets all have a floral design, usually with a central medallion on a field decorated by a motif of interlaced flowering branches. Some examples have also four corner decorations which have the same motifs and colours as

155

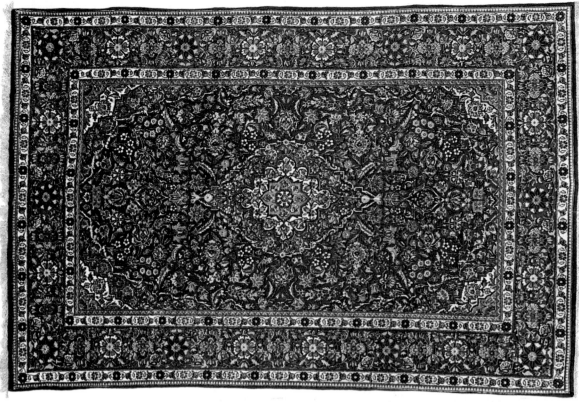

above: *Traditional Kashan carpet. Both decoration and colours of this specimen are typical of the Kashan district*

right: *Rare Kashan Motashemi carpet made in the second half of the nineteenth century. (Pars Collection, Milan)*

opposite page: *Kashan specimen, dating from the second half of the nineteenth century, decorated in border and field alike with the boteh motif. (Private Collection, Bolzano)*

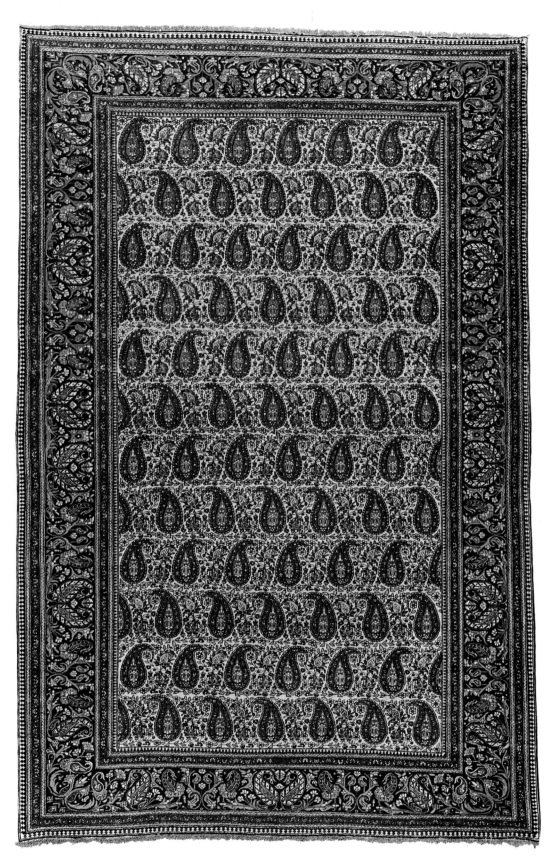

those used for the central medallion. Carpets with scenes of flowers and animals are also quite common. Another decoration which is typical of this area is the one known as 'vase of flowers'. The field of this carpet has at the bottom a vase from which flowering branches emerge and cover the whole of the field. In these examples, the field is often in the form of a niche, and therefore there are two quarters at the top of the niche at the opposite end from the vase.

The border of Isfahan carpets is usually made up of a large central band framed by two narrow guards which, in turn, are enclosed between two even narrower bands. The latter are almost always decorated with a Greek-key motif, while the two guards have a rosette motif joined by a garland.

The main border band often has a herati motif in a very elaborate form. In carpets with a decoration of plants and animals the ground motifs are repeated in the border.

A very wide colour range is used in Isfahan carpets and the ustad were masters at creating a harmonious combination of ground and design by alternating light and dark colours. (See illustrations on page 175.)

JOSHAQAN

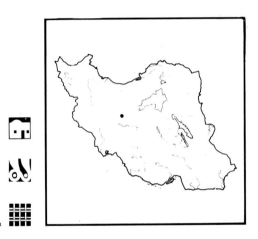

Cotton

PROVENANCE Village situated in the centre of Iran about halfway between Isfahan and Teheran. Joshaqan lies in a mountainous region and is surrounded by vast plantations of poplars.

opposite page: *Nineteenth-century Kashan Motashemi. This rare specimen belongs to a group of the first carpets made in Kashan in the Motashemi period. (Pars Collection, Milan)*

159

Kashan. Scene with figures, in silk. A Persian legend is inscribed along the three bands of the border

TECHNICAL DETAILS   The loom is vertical, warp and weft in cotton, pile in wool cropped low or medium. The Persian knot is used with a density varying between 80 and 160 knots to the square inch. The usual shape is sedjadeh.

DESCRIPTION   The decoration of Joshaqan carpets has remained unchanged for more than two centuries. At the Victoria and Albert Museum in London a fragment of a Joshaqan carpet from the seventeenth century is on show. This has a design very similar to those used for Joshaqans produced in modern times. The Joshaqan motifs consist of various designs of equal size depicting stylized flowers, leaves and flowering branches. The design as a whole forms a diamond shape and these flowering diamonds are arranged one beside the other to cover the whole field. In some specimens there is a diamond shaped medallion in the centre of the field which is outlined by a Greek-key motif usually in white. The medallion is also decorated with a Joshaqan motif and is made to stand out from the rest of the ground by the different colour of the background (usually a red ground and a blue medallion). Other examples have four triangular corner designs outlined by a white Greek-key pattern. The border is composed of a series of narrow guards and a large central band decorated with large flower and leaf motifs. The finest quality modern Joshaqan carpets are usually called Murcecar, from the name of a neighbouring village. Joshaqan designs are sometimes used by the craftsmen from nearby Kashan. (See illustrations on pages 171 and 172.)

KASHAN

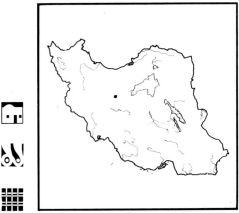

Cotton

PROVENANCE   Town of Kashan and the neighbouring villages such as Arun, Natanz and Nasirabad.

Kashan is situated some 150 miles to the south of Teheran on the edge of the Salt Desert. The summer is long and torrid with the temperature rising to above 50°C in the shade. Vegetation is practically non-existent because of the scarcity of water. To protect themselves from the heat the inhabitants of Kashan build downwards, living in houses of up to three levels below ground. These dwellings are ventilated by means of a large chimney divided into two parts which causes there to be a continuous circulation of air.

TECHNICAL DETAILS   Vertical loom; warp and weft in cotton; short cut good quality wool pile. The Persian knot is used and the density varies between 130 and 350 knots to the square inch. There are quite a number of examples which are made completely in silk, warp, weft and pile. These have as many as 600 knots to the square inch.

The usual sizes are: sedjadeh 4ft–4ft 6in × 6ft–7ft; qali 7ft–8ft × 10ft 6in–11ft; 10ft 3in–11ft × 13ft 6in–14ft 6in.

DESCRIPTION   After the Court period which culminated with the reign of Shah Abbas, carpet-making in Kashan was interrupted for more than two centuries between the Afghan invasion in 1722 and the end of the nineteenth century. It was only during the last quarter of the nineteenth century that some textile mill owners, finding themselves in difficulties because of competition with imported textiles, decided to try launching the carpet-making trade again.

The first examples woven after this renewed beginning of the trade are noticeable for the magnificent quality of the wool which makes the carpets

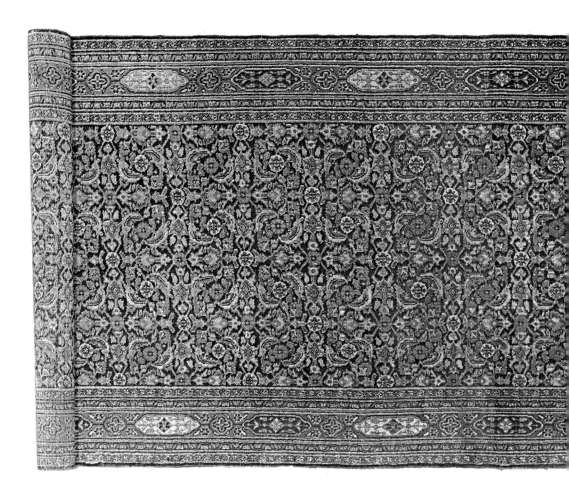

left: *Khorassan carpet of recent manufacture decorated with a floral motif*

below: *Early nineteenth-century Khorassan stair carpet. Note that the herati motifs of the field do not have the rhombus around the rosette*

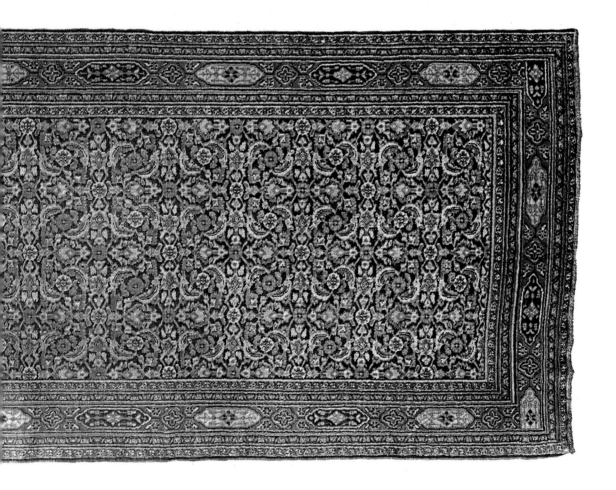

extremely velvety. It would appear that these examples were made with wool imported from Australia and which was used for making very highly priced materials. These carpets are known as Kashan Motashemi, probably from the name of one of the first craftsmen. In a few years, because of the very high quality of the wool, the very fine weaving and the beautiful colours and designs, Kashans came to be classified among the finest of the Persian carpets. Modern production has also kept up a high level and has maintained the world prestige of these carpets. Kashans are easily recognizable by their design. The field is almost always decorated by a central medallion which terminates at the upper and lower ends in flowering coronets. The rest of the field is closely decorated with flowers and vine tendrils. In the four quarters a richly decorated band outlines a motif which recalls the designs and colours of the central medallion. Kashans without a medallion are much rarer. These have a floral decoration accompanied by a decoration including animals such as the giraffe and peacock. The border is made up of two or four guards flanking the central one, which is always decorated with a herati border motif, while the guards have the usual decoration of rosettes and a garland.

Another fairly common type of Kashan is that with a figural decoration – story carpets – which are almost always in silk. One of these silk story carpets is illustrated on page 160. The border contains the story of a Persian legend, and the field illustrates one of the scenes. It tells of a Persian prince who, with a single arrow, transfixed the ear and leg of a doe, as he had wagered his wife that he would. But she, rather than congratulating him upon his skill, argued that this was no more than his usual skill in hunting. The prince was angered and has his wife shut up in a castle. After a long time, the prince was passing the tower and was astonished to see his imprisoned wife climbing the tower with an ox on her shoulders. He questioned her and discovered that she had succeeded in doing this by training herself each day with this exercise since the ox was a calf. The prince was won over, changed his mind, and took his wife back to his home. The carpet, which is about sixty years old, measures some 6ft 6in × 4ft 3in.

The usual background colours for Kashan carpets are brick red and dark blue. Very often the carpets with a dark blue background have medallion and border in red, and vice versa.

A recent kind of Kashan carpet, the pange-rangh (five colours) is, as its name implies, woven entirely in wools dyed in five colours. The background is generally ivory and the other colours are various shades of beige, grey and light blue. The pange-rangh also have a new decoration which consists of a geometric interpretation of the classic motifs of this area. (See illustrations on pages 156–158, 160.)

opposite page: *Typical late nineteenth-century Meshed carpet. The field decoration contains the islim motif*

164

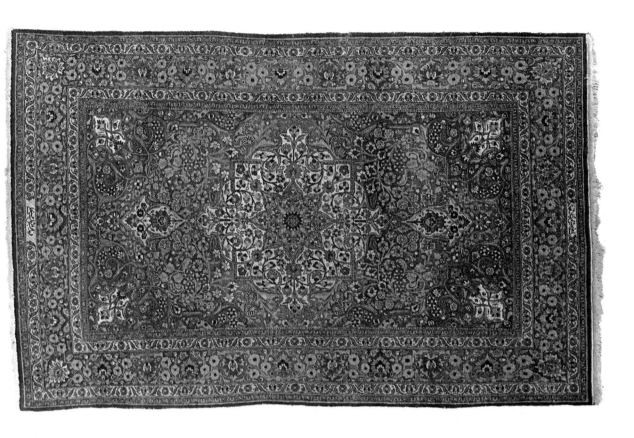

KERMAN
Yezd

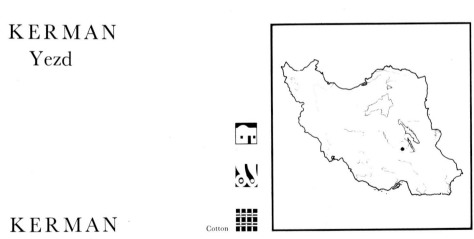

KERMAN

Cotton

PROVENANCE   Kerman carpets come from the city of the same name and from villages scattered over a range of some thirty miles from the main centre. Kerman is situated in south-east Iran in one of the most desolate zones of the whole country. Hundreds of miles of desert tableland separate it in every direction from the other centres to the south and the east. Some twenty-five miles from Kerman there is a most beautiful mausoleum dedicated to Shah Nima-

165

tullah, a fifteenth-century Dervish. The spatial harmony of the building, the richness of designs and the variety of colours demonstrate the innate talent of the artisans of Kerman who are well known as being the most skilful in the whole of Persia.

TECHNICAL DETAILS   Vertical loom; warp and weft in cotton; two rows of weft between each row of knots. The pile is in wool and may be either close- or medium close-cropped. Except for a few unusual cases, Kerman carpets can be divided into four qualities: 70, 80, 90 and 100. These four numbers correspond to the number of warp threads in a ghireh (one ghireh = about $2\frac{1}{2}$ inches). If you remember that each knot uses two warp threads you can easily calculate the number of knots to the square inch of any of these qualities. For example, one of the 70 quality has 196 knots to the square inch, i.e. $70 \div 2 = 35$ knots to the ghireh; $35 \div 2\frac{1}{2} = 14$ knots per inch; $14 \times 14 = 196$ knots to the square inch.

DESCRIPTION   Kerman carpets exist in all the classic Persian dimensions, though they are rarely found in the elongated kelley shape.

The success of Kerman carpets is due to a large extent to the skill of the cartoon designers (ustad). The ustad were able to unite their innate ability and aristic sensitivity to a respect for tradition. The result is that while all Kerman carpets have something in common which distinguishes them from those of other areas, they are made in a very, very wide range of designs. These designs often reveal Western influence. In fact, at the beginning of this century, some importers of carpets created new production centres and financed the craftsmen of Kerman. The ustad, for their part, adapted their designs to the demands of the European and American markets. Modern production is also divided into carpets destined for the United States, Europe and the home market. Each artisan is specialized in the manufacture of carpets for one of these destinations and makes only that kind of carpet, even though the difference between the various kinds is very small.

Kerman carpets are all in floral designs. Many have a rich central medallion which stands out against a self-colour background.

The motifs used for the medallions are used also in the border and in the corners. Some of these specimens are known by the name of ghab Korani, which

Magnificent nineteenth-century Kerman Ravar carpet. Although the decoration is a very rich one, a rare harmony is achieved by means of the balance between the decorations of the centre, the corners and the border. (Private Collection, Milan)

166

in Persian means Koran cover because the usual motifs used for decoration are those which used to be used for covers for the ancient Korans.

Other Kerman carpets, almost always in the 100 quality, have a field which is entirely covered by a very close floral design. Some examples retain the central medallion while in others the decoration is uniform over the entire field. Sometimes the ground decoration of Kerman carpets reveals the influence of Persian miniaturist art. These are examples decorated with flowers and animals and, more rarely, with figures in hunting scenes. The very few examples decorated with the tree of life are very beautiful. In this case the field is in the form of a niche. Another motif found in the decoration of Kerman rugs is the boteh. Very often this is one of the decorative elements, but occasionally it is used as a principal decoration. The border of Kerman carpets is usually composed of two rather narrow guards and a central band which is almost always decorated with designs similar to those used for the field.

168

opposite: *Nineteenth-century
Kerman Ravar. The almost square
shape and the proportion between
the decorative elements of the field
and the border give this carpet a
special character. (Private
Collection, Milan)*

above: *A modern Kerman carpet.
The motif used in this specimen is
known as ghab Korani (Koran
cover) from which this design is
derived*

KERMAN LAVER

DESCRIPTION   These are very beautiful carpets of Kerman design and quality
woven by the artisans of Ravar, a village situated some twenty-five miles from
Kerman where, by tradition, only carpets of very high quality are made.

Laver is a corruption of Ravar and so these carpets ought to be known as
Kerman Ravar carpets.

169

YEZD

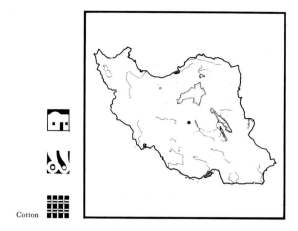

Cotton

DESCRIPTION   The town of Yezd situated about 150 miles to the west of Kerman, is known throughout Iran for the industriousness of its inhabitants, who are of Zoroastrian origin. Among the various craft activities practised at Yezd, the best known is silk and cotton weaving which is carried out on a hand loom. It is perhaps for this reason that until a few years ago the craft of carpet-making was practically non-existent. The inhabitants found that they made a better profit selling materials. Gradually, however, the local production dropped as imports increased and the craftsmen of Yezd turned to carpet-making. The decoration of Yezd carpets repeats the Kerman motifs, particularly that of the central medallion on a self-colour field. The technical details are also similar but usually the knot density is somewhat lower.

KHORASSAN
Meshed
Birjand

PROVENANCE   Vast region which extends from the central northern area of the Iranian Highlands to the borders with Afghanistan to the east and Russia to the north-east. The capital and principal centre of Khorassan is the city of Meshed which is situated less than sixty miles from the Russian frontier and some ninety miles from the Afghan border. Meshed is one of the most important towns in Iran and its principal mosque is a place of pilgrimage for Muslim Scythians. Another important town and centre of carpet-making is Birjand, situated about 240 miles to the south of Meshed. Near to Birjand is the village of Mud, also known for its carpet-making.

TECHNICAL DETAILS   Khorassan carpets can be divided into three groups: Khorassan, Meshed and Birjand.

170

KHORASSAN

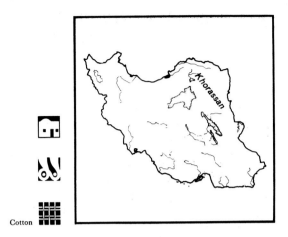

Cotton

DESCRIPTION   The term Khorassan is used for antique and old carpets from this area because recent production is identified both by decoration and technique with Meshed carpets. The famous herati design used in so many Persian carpets originated in this region and naturally constitutes the principal motif of Khorassan carpets. The name of herati derives from the Afghan town of Herat, the ancient capital of Khorassan but, contrary to common belief, carpets are no longer made at Herat. Antique Khorassan carpets are often called Herat carpets because they were sent to the West from that town.

The herati motif covers the whole field of Khorassan carpets, and it is interesting to note that the central rosette of the herati is not enclosed in a dimaond as is

Eighteenth-century Joshaqan. Its decoration shows how long the Joshaqan design persisted

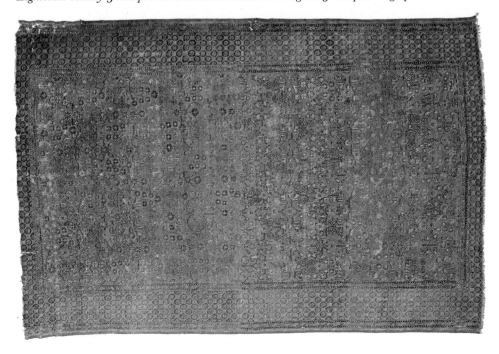

usual in examples which utilize this motif. In Khorassan carpets the herati is reproduced in its original form (see pages 162 and 163). The border is a succession of narrow bands, the guards decorated with rosettes or botehs, and the principal one decorated with border herati.

172

In some examples, particularly those from the eighteenth century, the boteh motif is used in the decoration of the border. Khorassan carpets are easily identifiable by a particular characteristic of their technique: the weft is normally formed by a single thread of cotton, but every seven to ten rows it is composed of three threads. This peculiarity can be seen on the back of the carpet where at regular intervals a clear line can be seen. The most common shapes of Khorassan carpets are the long ones or kelleys (5ft–8ft 3in × 9ft 10in–19ft 3in).

The colours vary according to the area. Orange shades and other bright colours are to be found in very great numbers in the carpets woven in the south of Khorassan, while in other areas the colours are duller and paler. Khorassan carpets come particularly from the region of Qainat situated to the south of Meshed, and particularly from the centres of Qayen and Dorokhsh.

MESHED

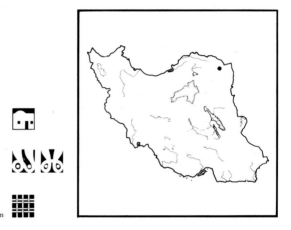

Cotton

DESCRIPTION   Meshed carpets can be divided into two groups: Meshed and Meshed Turkish. Both of these kinds are woven on vertical looms mostly grouped in small craft centres.

Warp and weft are in cotton; the number of knots varies from 100 to 200 to the square inch.

The difference between these two groups lies in the knot: the Meshed uses the Persian knot and the Meshed Turkish, as the name implies, the Turkish knot. Meshed Turkish carpets owe their origin to the initiative of a group of merchants from Tabriz who, in the last century, organized some carpet-making centres at Meshed. Both the Meshed and Meshed Turkish carpets use the floral design known as islim, i.e. snake. In fact, the whole field of Meshed carpets is covered with a very clear thin snake-like line which twists its way over the whole area. The central medallion is mostly round.

The colours are vivid with a great deal of red in them. The border is formed by two or more guards which are rather narrow and decorated with small floral motifs, and by a central wide band decorated either with the floral islim motif or with a floral motif which is often enclosed in a rectangular or diamond-shaped surround.

173

BIRJAND

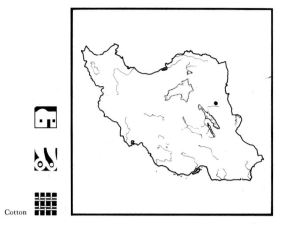

Cotton

DESCRIPTION   Birjand carpets are very similar to those from Meshed. Their decoration, however, is usually made up of the classic Persian floral design but with a round central medallion. Also the colours are similar to those of Meshed carpets and orange is used in the border and some of the field designs. In the nearby village of Mud, similar carpets are made which are identifiable by the fact that the field is generally self-coloured and the pile is rather thick.

LURISTAN

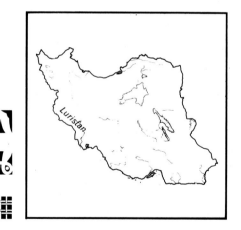

Wool

PROVENANCE   Carpets woven by Luri tribes living on the border between the Fars area and Luristan, in the south-west of Iran. The various Luri tribes come from the mountainous district of Luristan, famous for the civilization of the same name which dates back two thousand years before Christ.

opposite page, above: *Nine-teenth-century Isfahan. Its decoration is inspired by the antique Isfahan carpets of the Shah Abbas period*

below: *Late nineteenth-century Isfahan. It is decorated with a floral motif, with a central medallion, which is a classic design of this locality*

TECHNICAL DETAILS   The loom used is the nomad type, i.e. ground, or horizontal. Warp, weft and pile are always in very high quality wool. The knot used is Turkish and the number of knots per square inch varies between 50 and 80. The traditional size is about 5ft × 8ft 3in but quite a number are made in smaller sizes, particularly among tribes scattered towards the south. These carpets are called Behbehan and Kalardasht from the names of the villages which act as collecting centres. Large Luristan carpets are very rare.

DESCRIPTION   Like all nomad carpets, Luristans have a very simple geometric decoration. One of the commonest motifs from this locality is made up of three large diamonds placed one after the other along the central part of the carpet. These diamonds are often outlined with a Greek-key motif. The rest of the field decoration is composed of stylized flowering branches interspersed with large rosettes. The decoration is often completed by four triangular quarters.

Other carpets have a tree-of-life design which covers the whole field. Often there are two smaller trees, one on either side of the main one, symbolizing the continuance of life.

In other Luristan carpets the field is enclosed in a large hexagon decorated with small flowering branches arranged in diagonal lines. The border of these carpets is very simple and consists of three bands – two guards and a central, slightly wider, band decorated with motifs which echo those of the field. These are picked out on a different colour background, very often a pale colour. Luristan carpets are in fairly bright colours. The basic field colours are red and blue, while yellow, white and azure are common for the decoration.

NAIN

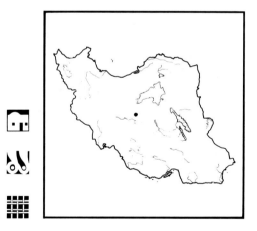

Cotton

PROVENANCE   Nain, a small town in the province of Isfahan, halfway between Isfahan and Yezd, is on the edge of the vast desert uplands of central Iran.

TECHNICAL DETAILS   Vertical loom. Warp and weft usually in very fine cotton. The weft passes twice between the rows of knots. The pile is normally in wool and is always very close-cropped. Silk is often used in the decoration also, and

Carpet made by the nomadic Luri tribe towards the end of the nineteenth century. The field decoration consists of plant motifs executed in straight lines

this particular mixture of materials serves to heighten the effect of some parts of the decoration. Some rare examples exist which are entirely of silk.

The Persian knot is used at a very high density – from 300 to 600 knots to the square inch.

Nain carpets are made in many different sizes, but a fairly common one is 5ft × 7ft 6in.

DESCRIPTION   Nain carpets, like those from Kashan, owe their origin to the decline of other crafts. Until the beginning of the twentieth century the main craft was the weaving of costly woollen cloth. This material was renowned for the high quality of the yarn which was hand-spun from best quality locally produced wool. However, when the Nain craftsmen saw the sales of their cloth falling as a result of imports of textiles from the West, they switched to carpet-making and, in a very few years, earned themselves a place among the quality carpet producers in Persia. The decoration of Nain carpets is similar to that used for Isfahans. Here, too, the field is decorated with an interlaced pattern of flowering branches. There are fewer carpets with a central medallion from Nain than there are from Isfahan.

Many Nain carpets have a decoration composed of plants and animals. The border is the traditional one of a wider central band flanked by two guards, sometimes framed by two narrow bands. All the bands are decorated with a floral motif, often enclosed in cartouches along the main one.

The colour scheme is typical of the region. Light colours are common for both background and decoration: beige, ivory and white, often alongside light green and azure, which is an alternative background colour.

A large proportion of Nain carpets are for the home market, where they are much appreciated, and for the Arab states.

opposite page: *Classic example of a Nain carpet of recent manufacture. The knot density reaches around 600 to the square inch*

178

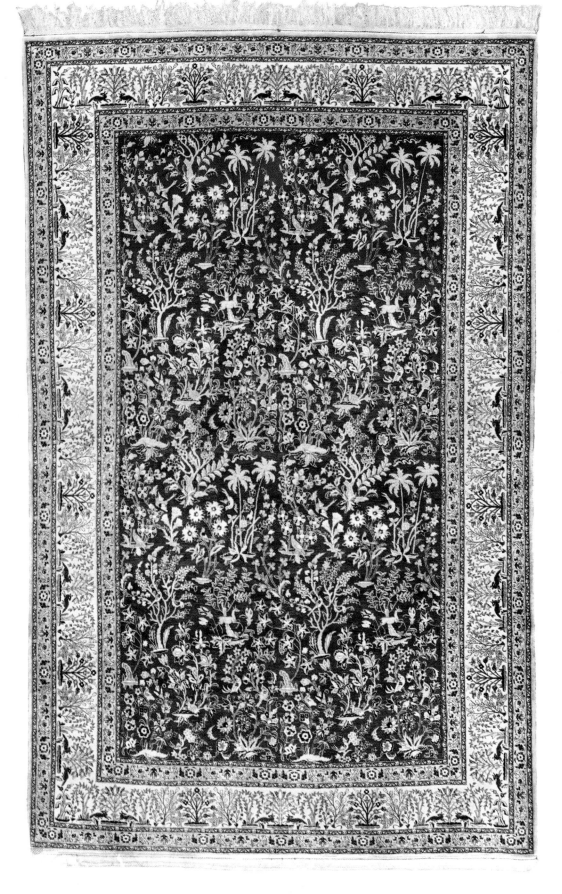

QUM

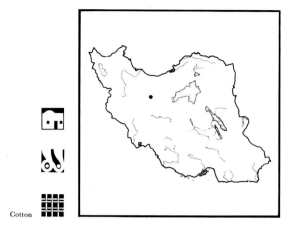

Cotton

PROVENANCE   Important city about ninety miles south of Teheran in a tolerably fertile part of the Iranian uplands and famous for its mosque with a gold cupola. It is a centre of pilgrimage for Scythian Muslims who come to pray at the tomb of Fatimah.

TECHNICAL DETAILS   Vertical looms, almost all concentrated in the city, in private homes, usually two to each house. Backing in cotton, with rare examples in silk. The pile is very often in wool, with an admixture of silk for the more detailed parts of some motifs. The weave is among the finest, with some 250–300 Persian knots to the square inch. The usual shapes are the sedjadeh and the qali, especially in the following sizes – 6ft 6in × 9ft 10in and 8ft 3in × 11ft.

DESCRIPTION   The first looms were set up at Qum in about 1930 as a result of the initiative of a group of merchants from Kashan. In spite of this late start, Qum rugs have taken their place among the best-known Persian carpets because of the high level of technique and the wide variety of patterns.

This rapid success is due in no small measure to the first cartoon designers who took up many Persian carpet ornamentations and worked on them to produce their patterns.

For example, the boteh motif, which originated in Mir carpets, is now associated with Qum. The zil-i-soltan motif, too, has become a classic Qum pattern. In addition, much use has been made of the Isfahan floral design with a self-colour ground and the Kashan central medallion design. Other Qum carpets are inspired by the Bakhtiari square design, though leaning towards a floral interpretation. The border – usually of three bands – is rather small in relation to the size of the carpet. The central band is often decorated with the ground motif but border herati is also quite common.

A vast range of colours is used for Qum carpets: white and ivory are the chief field colours, while the decoration is often in very vivid hues.

180

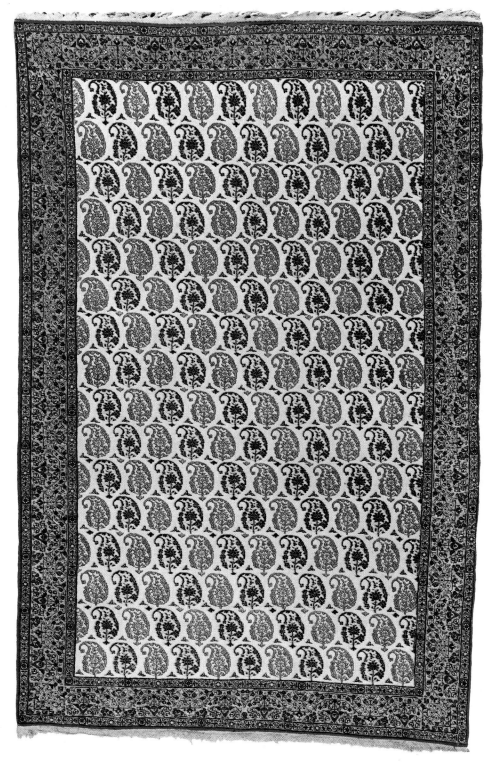

Qum with a field decoration of boteh motifs

SARUQ

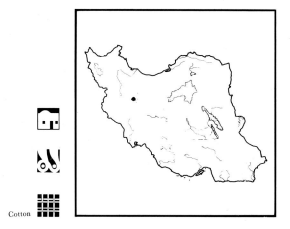

Cotton

PROVENANCE   These carpets originated in the village of Saruq in the agricultural district of Arak. For about thirty years they have also been woven in various other villages in the region and in the town of Arak.

below: *Modern Qum carpet. The field decoration is based on the zil-i-soltan motif*

opposite: *The originality of this Qum decoration is remarkable and owes nothing to inspiration from other quarters*

TECHNICAL DETAILS   Vertical loom; warp and weft in cotton. The weft consists of two or sometimes three threads of cotton. In carpets made before the First World War, the weft is pushed hard down against the knots, which made the carpets very compact. The pile is in very good quality wool. The pile is cut very short in the carpets originating from Saruq itself and in all the carpets dating from before 1920. More recent carpets, and particularly those made in Arak on order for American dealers, have a deeper pile.

The Persian knot is used and the density is always high – 160 to 400 knots to the square inch. Saruq carpets are made in all the classic Persian shapes except the runners. The most common form is the sedjadeh.

DESCRIPTION   Saruq decoration may be divided into two kinds: carpets with traditional designs and those intended for export, particularly to the United States of America.

The traditional decoration consists, for the most part, of the central-medallion pattern. The cartoons used are very like those used in Kashan, but the different interpretations by different craftsmen give the carpets a special imprint. Although Saruq carpets have a floral decoration, this is executed in an angular fashion, resulting in an incomparable fusion of sumptuous floral carpet decoration and primitive geometric styles. As well as the central-medallion design, there is also, in old and antique Saruq carpets, frequent use of the boteh motif. This is usually small in size and used as a repeating pattern over the whole ground. In these examples, the border is also often decorated with boteh.

In all Saruq carpets the border is simple, almost always consisting of two guards framing a wider central band. This band is often decorated with border herati, while the guards have the traditional rosette and wavy line decoration.

Varied colours are used for Saruq carpets. The field is often a bright orange-red, but this is often softened by the other colours, which are mainly ivory, dark blue, red-brown and dull green. Various shades of turquoise are common in the decorative motifs.

Carpets of recent manufacture, in particular those made at Arak, have a design which is clearly influenced by Western styles. The pattern used is a central medallion on a self-colour field which, in these carpets, is often pink, a background which blends with the delicate gradations of shades in the colours used for the designs.

These specimens are very similar to Kerman carpets intended for the American market.

Late nineteenth-century Saruq. The harmony of colour and the layout of the design combine to produce a remarkable effect

below: *Classic Saruq example with the characteristic central medallion. The origin of the design is clearly floral but it is treated in a linear fashion*

opposite: *A rare specimen from Saruq. Early nineteenth century. The field decoration is of simple motifs worked in lively colours. (Pars Collection, Milan)*

above and left: *Border and central medallion from an unusual nineteenth-century Saruq carpet. The designs and colours are peculiar to this locality*

SENNEH

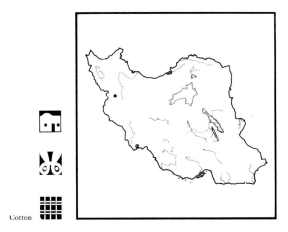

Cotton

PROVENANCE Senneh, the capital of Kurdistan, is a small town in a valley surrounded by fertile hills, particularly rich in vineyards.

TECHNICAL DETAILS Vertical looms set up only in the town itself. The backing is in cotton, or in silk for the finer carpets. In both cases the warp threads are very fine and are tightly spun. In spite of the common use of the term Senneh knot to indicate the Persian knot, it is, in fact, the Turkish knot which is used in Senneh carpets. The number of knots per square inch is very high and can reach 500. The short pile is always in wool. Senneh carpets are very light because of the fine warp and weft and short pile.

DESCRIPTION Although Senneh carpets are woven by Kurdish craftsmen, they differ substantially from other Kurdistan carpets. Kurdish carpets, in fact, have a wool weft, a deep, irregularly-cut pile and primitive designs. It would seem that the very fine work at Senneh came into being when Nadir Shah named Senneh the capital of Kurdistan and sent a governor and other dignitaries to live there. They despised Kurdish carpets and ordered the craftsmen of the town to weave carpets for their houses which were much finer and which had a cotton warp. So the craftsmen of Senneh started to make fine quality carpets and over the centuries the tradition has been maintained. Senneh designs have remained unchanged also. The most frequently used motifs are the herati, which is used to cover the whole carpet, and the boteh.

If the design used is the central-medallion type, this is only distinguished by a different background colour (dark blue field, light medallion). The border is also decorated with herati.

The boteh, on the other hand, is used with more imagination than usual. In some carpets it is arranged in the customary vertical lines, though in this case the almond is usually rather large (8in). In other carpets the boteh are arranged in a circle and each one forms the petal of a rose. These roses are repeated to cover the field of the carpet. Another fairly common motif in Senneh carpets is the gul-i-Mirza Ali (flower of Mirza Ali). This particular type of Senneh has a herati border and, on the inside, a floral motif which clearly betrays its French origins.

189

Nineteenth-century kilim, Senneh.
It belongs to the group of weft-face
carpets which are made by using
the special techniques described on
page 129

Senneh borders are the traditional three-band type with the central one usually decorated with border herati in an extremely angular form. Border boteh is also quite usual, while some specimens have a floral-type decoration enclosed in small cartouches. Senneh carpets are usually either in dark colours, such as deep blue and wine, or in light, brilliant colours like ivory and yellow. The colours are always pleasing and harmonious.

Nineteenth-century Senneh. The field decoration of this example makes use of the motif known as gul-i-Mirza Ali, which is reminiscent of French decorative motifs

following page: *A very unusual Senneh carpet from the early nineteenth century. The knotting is done on a silk warp. The field decoration is of lines of boteh motifs and is surrounded by the herati border motif. (Pars Collection, Milan)*

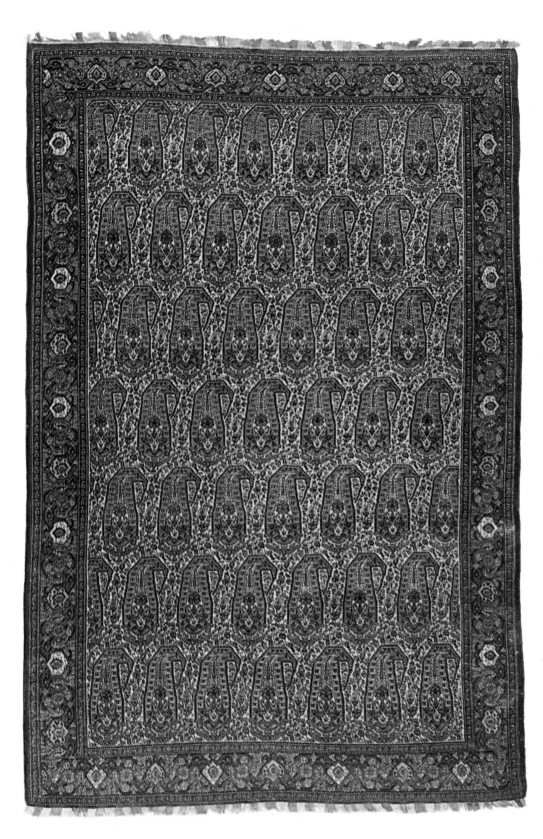

SERABAND
MIR

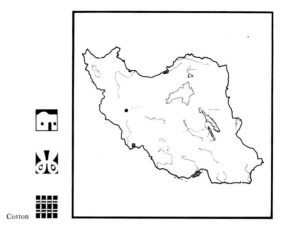

Cotton

PROVENANCE   Mountainous region to the south of the town of Arak and to the east of Borujerd. The carpets from this locality are woven in some thirty Seraband villages. For several decades Seraband carpets have also been woven in Arak.

TECHNICAL DETAILS   Vertical loom. Warp and weft are in rather coarsely spun cotton. There are two warps between the rows of knots and the warp threads are often dyed pale blue which makes them easily seen on the reverse of the carpet. The pile is in wool, either local yarn or obtained from the Luri tribesmen in Borujerd. The finest carpets are made with this latter type of wool. The Turkish knot is used and the average number of knots per square inch is 100. The most common shape is the runner, or kelley.

DESCRIPTION   Before describing Seraband carpets, it is perhaps a good moment to speak of Mir carpets, which were their predecessors. The origin of Mir carpets is more legend than history. It is said that these carpets, much appreciated in England and rare nowadays, were woven in the village of Mal-e-Mir, chief town of the Seraband district. Mal-e-Mir means Mir's property, and Mir is a title which the Persians reserve for the descendants of Mohammed and for persons of high standing and ability. The very fine workmanship and the pleasing decoration of these carpets may therefore be attributable to the special skill of the craftsmen who made them. Mir carpets are easily identifiable because of their design, called boteh-mir. This is probably the first of the multitude of varied applications of this motif.

In Mir carpets the boteh is very small (2in–4in) and is outlined by small angled lines rather than by curves. In other examples the boteh does not have an outside edge but is formed by large numbers of tiny flowers in an almond shape. The background of Mir carpets is usually dark, often blue, whilst the designs are in various colours, the most conspicuous being a very beautiful golden yellow. The border is richly decorated and is made up of a series of parallel strips.

Seraband carpets have kept the boteh-mir. Some examples have a unique variant in the form of a central diamond-shaped medallion, decorated with

193

194

Seraband stair carpet made towards the middle of the 1800s. The boteh motif decorates both the field and the principal band of the border. (Pars Collection, Milan)

boteh, and four quarters which repeat the colours of the border designs. The border itself consists of a number of narrow bands in alternating colours, decorated with geometric motifs and border boteh alternating with a self-colour wavy line.

The colours used for the field in Seraband carpets are more numerous than in Mir carpets. As well as blue, there are examples with red, pink and ivory backgrounds as well.

Although Seraband carpets are far from being of as excellent a quality as Mir carpets, they are pleasant and extremely durable.

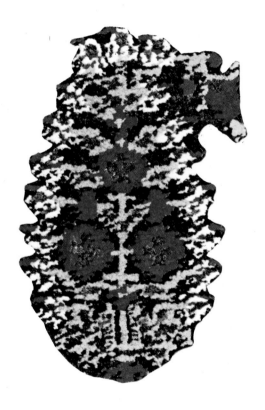

above, left: *boteh motif, actual size. (Private Collection, Verona)*

opposite: *A rare Mir specimen made in the Seraband area in the first half of the nineteenth century. The field decoration is the boteh motif in its original form*

196

SHIRAZ
Kashkay

SHIRAZ

PROVENANCE   Contrary to what one might expect, Shiraz carpets are not made in Shiraz itself but in the whole Fars area of which Shiraz is the capital. The various carpets known by this name are, in fact, woven by different nomadic tribes which have lived for centuries on the Fars tableland. The bazaar in the town of Shiraz is the trading centre for these carpets.

TECHNICAL DETAILS   Ground looms are used even for the carpets woven by the semi-nomadic people living in small Fars communities. Warp and weft are in wool except for some types woven by semi-nomadic people who use cotton. The weft can be either single or double, according to the tribe, but the pile is always in wool. Some tribes use the Persian knot, others use the Turkish. In both cases

Traditional Shiraz carpet made by the nomadic Fars tribe

the number of knots per square inch is rarely more than 100. However, it is impossible to be precise about the average knot density of Shiraz carpets because the quality varies enormously from tribe to tribe. The best carpets are those woven by the Arab and Basiri tribes, which are also known as Shiraz Extra.

The usual sizes of Shiraz carpets are 6ft 6in–8ft 3in × 9ft 10in–11ft 3in and 4ft 6in–6ft 3in × 6ft 6in–8ft 3in. Larger and smaller sizes than these are very rare.

DESCRIPTION   Shiraz decoration is typically nomad. The motifs are simple and geometric, executed in bold straight lines and bright colours. The most common motif and one by which a Shiraz carpet may be identified, is the diamond-shaped lozenge by itself in the centre of the carpet or repeated along the length twice or three times according to the size.

The diamond shape is usually light or dark blue and the field almost always red and decorated with stylized plant motifs. The border is nearly always made up of a number of narrow bands framing a wider band which is often decorated with a motif resembling palm or pine leaves. The edging bands are often separated from each other by a narrow band of diagonal stripes.

KASHKAY

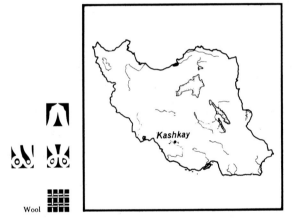

Wool

Although Kashkay carpets are included in the description of Shiraz carpets because of their common provenance (Fars) and similarity of design, they merit a separate mention.

These are carpets woven by the Kashkay tribe who live in the Fars uplands. The Kashkay peoples are the most developed of the Fars tribes. This more advanced development is reflected in the superiority of their carpets over Shiraz ones.

The wool used is selected and spun with greater care, the variety and quality of the colours are superior and the number of knots (Turkish) to the square inch higher. The result is a carpet which is harder wearing, with a compact pile and faster, more varied colours.

Kashkay carpet made towards the end of the nineteenth century. Its decoration is highly original, far removed from the motifs usually used in carpets from this district.

opposite: *Nineteenth-century Kashkay. The decoration is typical of the district*

200

*Shiraz. The field decoration
includes three medallions, as is
customary in carpets from this
locality*

As we have seen, the motifs are the same as for Shiraz carpets, though in some examples the columns of Cyrus's palace are represented between the field and the border. The Kashkay tribe often camps near Persepolis, the ancient Achaemenian capital.

TABRIZ
Heriz
Karaj

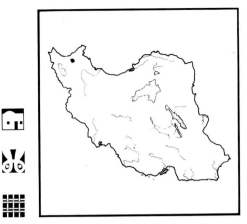

TABRIZ

Cotton

PROVENANCE   City situated in the north-west of Iran, close to the Russo-Turkish border. For many centuries Tabriz has been one of the most important towns in Persia. In the thirteenth century it was the capital of the Mongol Empire. Because of its geographical situation, Tabriz suffered a number of invasions but these, on the credit side, had an influence on the evolution of its people.

Tabriz lost its role as the main commercial centre of Persia only in the last thirty or so years since Shah Reza the Great caused all commercial activity to be centred on Teheran.

TECHNICAL DETAILS   Tabriz carpets come almost exclusively from the city itself and the majority are woven in production centres where there are quite a large number of looms. Relatively few carpets are made in private houses. The loom is vertical, often with metal roller beams. The Turkish knot is always used (the population of Tabriz is Turkish by both race and language). The backing is of very strong cotton with a double weft.

The pile is in wool which usually comes from the Maku region (on the border with Turkey) or from the Rizaiyeh lake area to the south-west of Tabriz. This wool is very strong but rather coarse, with the result that the pile, particularly in medium quality carpets, is uneven and rough.

At the beginning of the century, the finest carpets had a silk pile. These rare pieces are among the most beautiful examples of Persian carpet-craft.

Tabriz carpets are woven in six standard qualities: 25, 30, 35, 40, 50 and 60. These numbers represent the number of knots to a punzeh (about 3 inches). Quality 35, for example, has 144 knots to the square inch, i.e., $35 \div 3 = 12$ (approx.) knots to the inch: $12 \times 12 = 144$ knots to the square inch.

The usual sizes are sedjadeh and large carpets (6ft 6in × 9ft 10in and larger).

DESCRIPTION   Tabriz carpets play a very important role in Persian carpet production in general. It was at Tabriz, in fact, that carpets were first made for export. From the middle of the nineteenth century, the wily traders of Tabriz had been sending to Istanbul old carpets which they had picked up one by one from the houses of Persian nobles. They soon realized that demand greatly

203

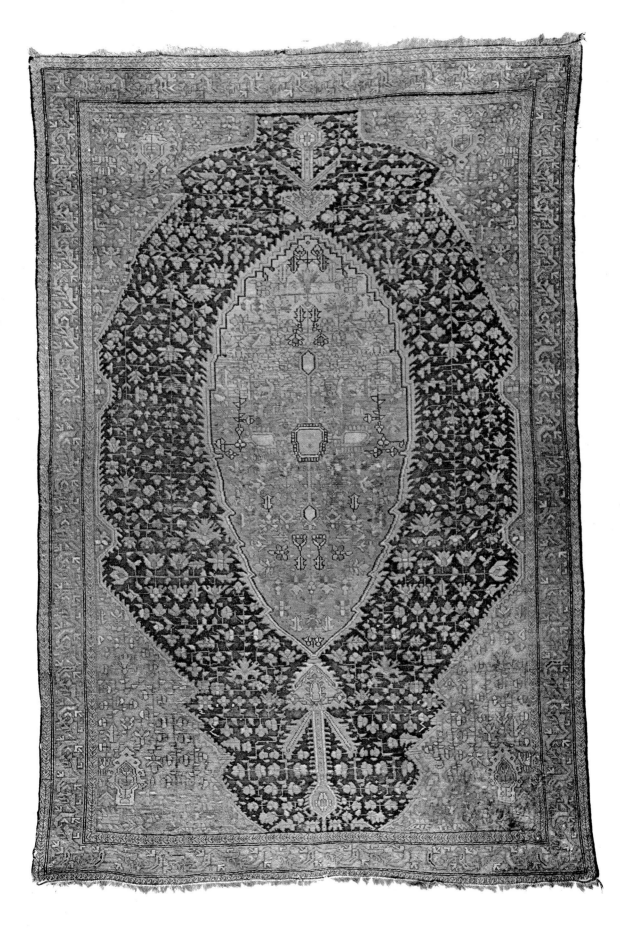

exceeded supply and decided to turn themselves from traders into producers. So it was that the first carpet-making centres were set up where carpets were made in the sizes and colours required for the European market. It is perhaps for this reason that there is no particular colour associated with Tabriz. The decoration is floral, often with a central medallion. The motifs — flowering

branches, shrubs and leaves – are large. In addition to these classic themes, plant and animal motifs also appear in some Tabriz carpets. Specimens decorated with the herati motif are rarer.

The border is usually composed of three guards and a main band decorated either with a repetition of the ground motifs or with border herati.

HERIZ

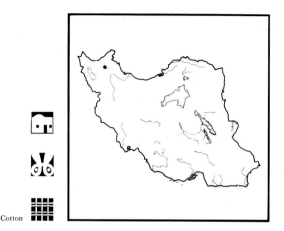

Cotton

DESCRIPTION   Although Heriz carpets belong to the Tabriz family, they merit a special mention because of some peculiarities in the techniques used. These carpets come from some thirty villages within a radius of about thirty miles from Tabriz. The most important of these are Heriz, Georavan, Bakshaish and Mehraban.

Heriz carpets have much in common with those from Tabriz, in particular the use of the Turkish knot. Also, the cartoons used are the same: but they are interpreted by the village craftsmen in a very different way. The craftsmen of Heriz, in fact, do not know how to weave in curvilinear patterns and transform the arabesques of the cartoon into perpendicular, horizontal and diagonal lines. So, two different kinds of carpet can result from the use of the same design. The Tabriz carpet will be classic and sophisticated, the Heriz simple and stylized. European connoisseurs are cognizant, not only with the name of Heriz, but also with that of Georavan which is used to indicate carpets of ancient manufacture from this district. Georavan carpets usually have a light background and splendid decorative motifs in shades ranging from burnt chestnut to midnight blue.

opposite page: *This Heriz carpet, which has been given a reduction wash, is decorated with the traditional motifs of the district*

208

KARAJ

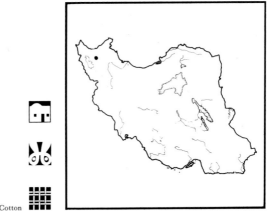

Cotton

DESCRIPTION Karaj rugs also belong to the Tabriz sphere of influence but merit a special note, too. These are usually small rugs (sedjadeh) or runners, woven in the village of Karaj which lies to the north-east of Tabriz on the Tabriz-Ahar road.

The techniques used are the same as those in Tabriz with the sole difference that they have a single warp. The wool used for these rugs is superior in quality to the average Tabriz wool and the result is a closer-cropped, more uniform pile.

Karaj rugs are easily recognizable from their design, which consists of three medallions. The two side medallions are the same size as each other and of the same colour as the field. The central medallion is larger and of a different colour, mostly dark blue. The two side medallions resemble the eight-pointed star in shape, while the central one is diamond-shaped, often with an outline of running-dog motifs. The internal decoration of the medallions is completed by geometric plant motifs.

Karaj runners are decorated with the same motifs but, because of the long shape, the sequence of medallions is different.

The dyes used for Karaj carpets are sober but pleasing: bottle green, tan and yellow ochre.

Late nineteenth-century Karaj stair carpet. The ornamentation of the field is achieved by using motifs typical of the district. Serrated leaves decorate the border

VERAMIN
Teheran

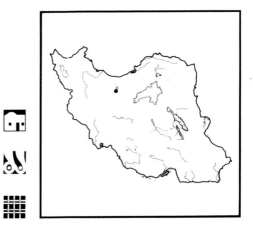

VERAMIN

Cotton

PROVENANCE   Veramin carpets are made in the village of the same name situated in an agricultural area some sixty miles to the south of Teheran.

TECHNICAL DETAILS   The loom is vertical, the backing is tightly spun cotton. The Persian knot is used and the density varies between 220 and 330 knots to the square inch.
   The most usual shape is 6ft 6in–7ft 6in × 9ft 10in–11ft 3in.

DESCRIPTION   The field decoration of Veramin carpets consists almost exclusively of three motifs, described on the next page.

VERAMIN ZIL-I-SOLTAN:

The classic vase-of-flowers motif, which is one of the most frequent and pleasing motifs in Persian carpets, is used in rather large dimensions in Veramin carpets, as in those from Abadeh, but, because of the high knot density, the execution is exact in every detail.

The resulting decoration is made even more delightful by the happy choice of colour scheme: red, green and grey, usually on an ivory background for the motif.

VERAMIN MINA KHANI:

The mina-khani motif is composed of four flowers of equal size arranged in a diamond. The inside of the diamond is decorated either with a large flower similar to the four external ones, or of five daisies, one large one in the centre and four smaller ones around it.

All in all, these carpets, which resemble a field of flowers, are very attractive.

The field colours of these Veramin carpets are usually midnight blue or dark red and the flowers are in bright, harmonious shades.

PLANT AND ANIMAL VERAMIN:

As the name clearly implies, the decoration of these carpets consists of closely interwoven flowering branches and shrubs with a haphazard scattering of numerous animal figures. Lions and stags are among the animals most fre-

This Veramin specimen, like many carpets from the same area, is decorated with the floral motif called mina khani

quently depicted. The decoration as a whole is clearly inspired by sixteenth-century Persian miniaturist art. The range of colours used in this decoration is very wide, an indispensable concomitant of such varied decorative motifs.

The borders, like those in carpets from other parts of Iran, is small in relation to the field. The basic pattern is of a central border band framed by two guards outlined by narrower bands.

These narrow bands are almost always decorated by a series of indentations formed by a small triangle and with a diamond above, sharing a common vertex. The decoration of these bands is important as it serves to distinguish Veramin and Teheran carpets from others with a similar field decoration (Qum, for example). The two guards have quite a varied decoration: the one which occurs most frequently is the twining branch interspersed with rosettes.

The central band is mostly decorated with the motifs used for the field, but in some specimens border herati is employed.

One important characteristic is that the background colour of the border is usually the same as that used for the field.

TEHERAN

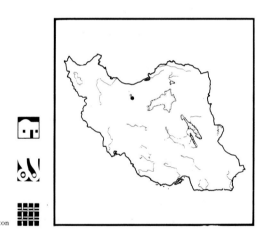

Cotton

DESCRIPTION   Teheran carpets have not been made for some decades because labour costs in the Persian capital are too high nowadays.

Old and antique Teheran carpets have the same decoration as modern Veramins. Of the three Veramin designs, the most frequently used in these old carpets was the floral and animal pattern. Teheran carpets are of very fine quality and the colours sober but pleasing.

Another common Teheran decoration was the vase of flowers already described in the section on Isfahan. These carpets, too, have a niche-shaped field. These specimens are much prized by connoisseurs and are practically beyond price nowadays.

213

Nineteenth-century Teheran. The extremely delicate technique used for this carpet enabled the zil-i-soltan motif to be used in a very small size while still leaving the design clear in every detail.
(Private Collection, Verona)

TURKESTAN AND
AFGHANISTAN

Bukhara Samarkand

Yomud

Hadklu

Beshir

Kerki

Kizyl Ajak

Pendeh

KABUL

HERAT

Afghan

Firdaus

Baluchistan

AFGHAN

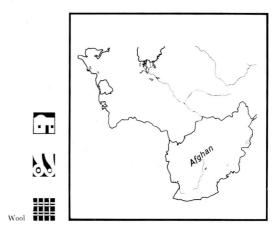

Wool

PROVENANCE   Afghan carpets are woven in a vast area which includes the provinces of Turkestan and Afghanistan. Originally nomad carpets, they are now woven in craft centres.

TECHNICAL DETAILS   The warp and weft is in wool – often goat's wool, as can be seen from the greyish colour of the fringe. The pile is in good quality wool which has quite a sheen and may be of medium or deep pile according to where the carpet was made.

Some nineteenth-century specimens have a short pile and these are carpets with a high knot density. Afghan carpets are usually made with the Persian knot at between 60 and 160 knots to the square inch.

They are made in almost all sizes but the customary ones are approximately 7ft 6in × 9ft 10in and 8ft 9in × 11ft 6in. As the measurements indicate, Afghan carpets tend to be squarish in shape.

DESCRIPTION   Afghans are easily identifiable by design and colours. The decoration consists of a line of gul (see Bukhara). In these carpets the gul is much larger and more angular than it is in Bukhara carpets and is decorated with very simple motifs. The outer line of the motif forms a large octagon which encloses a centre polygon or square, while the rest of the gul is divided into four sections decorated with the same design. The gul are arranged in line at some distance from each other. Between the lines there are often stylized branches

opposite page : Afghan carpet of modern manufacture decorated with the traditional gul motif

216

terminating in geometric-style flowers. The border consists of a succession of narrow bands frequently decorated with simple geometric figures including the hooked Greek-key and serrated-leaf motifs.

The colours used are unmistakable: both field and border are in various shades of warm dark red. This colour is also used for the gul and border, along with different shades of red-brown, dark blue and black. Afghans have achieved considerable popularity in the West, chiefly because of their restrained colours and simple decoration.

BALUCHI

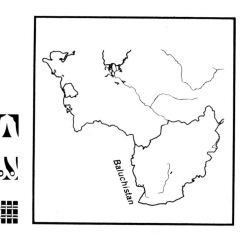

Wool

PROVENANCE   These rugs, contrary to the implication in the name, do not come from Baluchistan which is on the border between south-west Persia and Pakistan.

They are woven, in fact, in the eastern part of Khorassan and in a large area of western Afghanistan, along the Iranian border.

Baluchi rugs are almost exclusively nomad work and are woven, for the most part, by Baluchi tribes. A small number are woven by peoples of Arab origin living in the towns of Firdaus (central Khorassan) and the neighbouring villages.

TECHNICAL DETAILS   Like all nomad rugs, Baluchi rugs are made on ground looms, including those which come from Firdaus and the nearby villages.

The backing is mainly in wool though recently cotton has come into use as well. With a few exceptions, the weft is single. The pile is of good quality wool but is lacking in lustre and is not very deep. Natural camel wool is often used.

The knot used is Persian at between 60 and 100 knots per square inch. Normally, Baluchi rugs are small, like prayer rugs (2ft 6in–3ft 3in × 4ft–5ft 6in). There are, however, some old carpets which are larger.

DESCRIPTION   The commonest type of Baluchi rug is the prayer rug. Often the only common feature is the oriented form of the design. The differences lie in the multiplicity of motifs used which differ greatly from rug to rug. The most

218

This particular type of Baluchi carpet, with its elongated shape and with the field oriented differently from that of the Baluchi prayer rugs, comes from the region of Turbat-i-Haidari, situated to the south of Meshed

Baluchi prayer rug. The niche is decorated with a stylized tree of life. The field colour is that of undyed camel hair

Baluchi prayer rug. The decoration in this example is limited to simple geometric designs and some linked-hook patterns

frequently found design has a cupola on either side of the niche. In other Baluchi rugs, the field of the niche contains a tree of life.

Yet other examples have a more formal decoration which is frequently reduced to a simple division of the ground into diamonds of different colours.

Even the Baluchi rugs with a normal decoration use quite varied motifs – the typical ones used for rugs from this region as well as ones borrowed from elsewhere, such as the Bukhara gul or the floral mina khani. Baluchi borders are usually composed of a succession of narrow bands, almost all of the same size.

The border decoration is very simple and inspired by geometric designs, particularly the Greek key and diagonal wedges in alternating colours. Different colours are often used for each of the narrow bands but the wide one is always the same colour as the ground.

However different in design, Baluchi rugs have one point in common – the colours. Red and dark blue predominate, both of them used for field, motifs and borders. White, too, plays an important part, so much so that in some specimens the harmonious effect of the whole is spoilt by the over-enthusiastic use of this colour. Some Baluchi rugs have a beige ground – this is nearly always the result of the use of natural camel.

Yellow and orange are also quite common in the border and motifs.

BESHIR

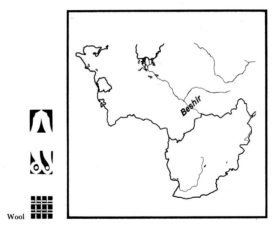

Wool

PROVENANCE   Carpets woven by Turkoman nomads living in the border regions between Turkmenistan, Uzbekistan and Afghanistan. The name Beshir comes from a small town to the south of Bukhara near to the Amu Darya river, which was probably the trading centre for these carpets.

TECHNICAL DETAILS   Warp and weft in wool with two weft threads between the rows of knots. Medium deep wool pile. Persian knot at between 60 and 160 per square inch. Beshirs are usually rather large and long (e.g. 5ft 10in × 9ft 10in). Even larger ones are quite common (e.g. 8ft–9ft 10in × 18ft–25ft 3in).

DESCRIPTION   Beshir carpets may be distinguished from other carpets woven

221

by Turkoman nomads in the Trans-Caspian area both by the decorative characteristics and by certain shades of colour typical of the region. Beshir designs are not, in fact, as rigidly geometric and stylized as those from neighbouring areas.

In both field and borders there are, quite frequently, small motifs and rosettes or octagons decorated with distinctly floral designs. Sometimes the field contains the herati motif, recognizable only by the lozenge, because the flowers and palmettes are rather different from the basic design and reveal the influence of motifs used in carpets from nearby Samarkand.

Beshir borders are rather special, too. The commonest form is that of a succession of narrow bands with alternating background colours (often red and yellow) and decorated with Turkoman geometric motifs (very often the hooked Greek-key motif).

In Beshir carpets with the herati motif the border contains this decoration as well. Here, as in the field, the motif is interpreted in an original way which reflects some Far Eastern influence.

The background colour of Beshir carpets is usually dark blue, but the motifs in red are so close together that the overall colour of the carpets appears to be red.

A colour characteristic of these carpets is a very vivid yellow which is used in the border and to outline some of the field motifs. The yellow contrasts with the darker shades of red and blue, and gives the carpets a gay appearance which is rather unexpected in Turkoman carpets.

opposite page: *A rare specimen of Beshir work from the first half of the nineteenth century. The field decoration is of tiny tightly packed herati motifs, while the splendid border work is typical of the Turkoman area. (Pars Collection, Milan)*

BUKHARA
Pinde
Kizyl-Ayak
Kerki

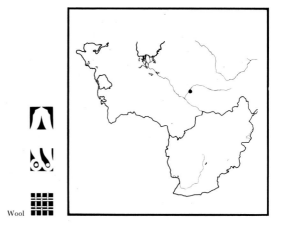

Wool

PROVENANCE   Bukhara carpets are not woven in that city but in a huge tract of land which includes Turkmenistan and Uzbekistan. These carpets are in fact made by nomads and, for the greater part, by the Turkoman tribe of the Tekkeh who live on the Trans-Caspian steppes. The name Bukhara was probably given to these carpets because of the position of the city, situated on the border between Turkmenistan and Uzbekistan, and because of the importance of this Muslim centre in centuries past. Bukhara carpets were probably sold by the nomad tribes in the famous bazaar of Bukhara.

TECHNICAL DETAILS   Wool warp and weft. The weft thread is very fine and is invisible even when used double. The pile is also in wool of excellent quality – soft, silky and hard-wearing. The quality of the wool is, in fact, one of the reasons why Bukhara carpets are so famous. The Persian knot is used with a very high density – between 160 and 320 knots per square inch.

Bukharas are made in almost all sizes. The most common are 4ft–4ft 3in × 6ft–6ft 3in and 6ft 6in–8ft × 9ft 10in–11ft.

DESCRIPTION   The motif used for Bukhara carpets is by far and away the best-known of all those used for decorating Oriental carpets. There are several reasons for this fame. Firstly there is the recognized beauty of Bukhara carpets which are prized to such an extent by Western dealers that they add the adjective Royal to the name. Then there is the simplicity and uniformity of the design which is repeated without significant modification in all the examples. Finally, Bukhara carpets are famous because their motif is used on so many carpets from other sources.

There are, in fact, in existence carpets which do not come from Turkestan but which use the gul (rose) of Bukhara. These include carpets woven by the Yomut nomads in North Gurgan (north-east Iran); by the Baluchi tribes of Khorassan, also in north-east Iran; and, for some decades, by Pakistanis in various parts of Pakistan.

Gul, the name of the typical Bukhara motif, means rose in Persian. It is an octagonal motif with slightly rounded angles. The four sides which are perpendicular to each other, are joined by four lines which, instead of being straight

224

above: *This modern carpet shows the typical Pinde motif. It comes from Pakistan*

below: *This is also a Pinde, woven in Turkestan in the second half of the nineteenth century*

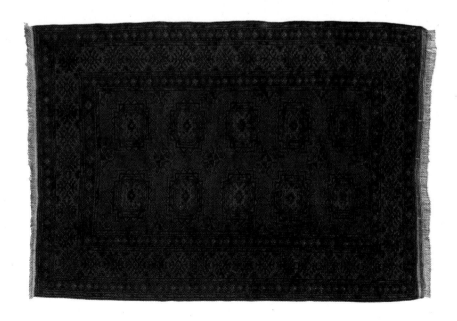

are slightly curved. In the inside of the gul is a motif made up of a combination of two rectangles joined together to form a large star with eight small points.

The gul is divided into four equal parts by two perpendicular lines which run the whole length and width of the carpet. Each part is distinguished from the next by a change of colour (one part in blue, black or, rarely, green, the next part red or orange). The band between the outer edge and the central motif is wholly in ivory or alternating ivory and light red. The gul, known also as 'elephant's foot' are arranged in a number of regular lines to cover the entire ground.

Between one line of gul and the next there is, in the field of Bukhara carpets, a cross-shaped motif the points of which branch out into a shape like the antennae of a butterfly. This motif also is arranged in regular lines.

Bukhara borders are usually formed by three bands, two narrow guards and a wide central band. This latter is decorated with octagons in alternating colours, generally blue and ivory.

The border of the head of the carpet is narrower and is preceded by a band decorated with either serrated leaves arranged diagonally, or by a lozenge motif outlined with a hooked Greek key.

The ground and border colour is almost always red, but in different shades, ranging from violet to orange. Bukharas with an ivory or dark blue background are very rare.

Grouped with Bukhara carpets are some others woven by nomadic tribes from the same region: Pinde, Kizyl-Ayak and Kerki.

Pinde carpets are most like Bukharas. Their special feature is a Greek-key outline to the gul. This motif is also quite common in Pakistani carpets.

Kizyl-Ayak, which means golden foot, are distinguishable by the larger size of the gul motif. The outer edge of the gul in this case is more rounded and shows a slight indication of influence of curvilinear patterns.

Kerki carpets, by contrast, are extremely formal; the ground is almost always decorated exclusively with stylized gul.

The specimen reproduced on the two preceding pages is a rare Bukhara carpet from the first half of the nineteenth century. These carpets are known in Europe as Royal Bukharas. (Pars Collection, Milan)

BUKHARA
PAKISTAN

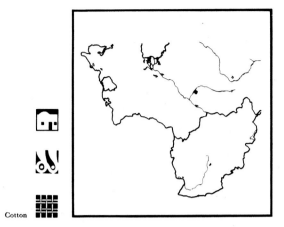

Cotton

The Bukhara carpets of Pakistan merit particular mention considering how widely they have become known throughout the West.

The warp and weft are in cotton, the pile is very very silky wool, often imported ready-spun from England. Pakistan carpets are very fine and may reach extremely high knot densities – from 400 to 500 per square inch. The price of these carpets is very reasonable because of the very low cost of local manpower and because of the aid given to exporters by the Pakistan Government. These carpets, however, have no tradition behind them and, on the whole, have a rather cold, unoriginal appearance.

HADKLU

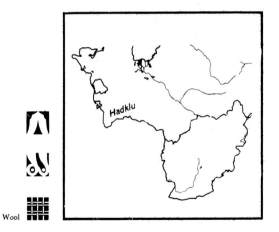

Wool

PROVENANCE   Hadklu rugs, like Bukharas, are woven by nomadic tribes living in Turkmenistan and Uzbekistan. The name Hadklu is not associated with any particular place but serves to indicate a type of prayer rug woven by various Turkoman tribes. Hadklu-type prayer rugs are widely known among the Yomut and Tekkeh tribes.

229

TECHNICAL DETAILS   Warp and weft in wool; short-cropped pile also in high quality wool. The techniques are in every way similar to those used for Bukhara carpets. The Persian knot is used and the density per square inch varies from 165 to 330. Hadklu rugs are almost unique as far as size goes and fall within the following sizes: 3ft 6in–4ft × 4ft 6in–5ft 6in.

DESCRIPTION   The principal motif of the Hadklu consists of a large cross which divides the field into four equal parts. The upper part of the cross ends in a point and the rug therefore has a point of orientation. In other specimens the cross is of the usual kind, and, in this case, there is a small niche (mihrab) included in the upper border of the rug. These special motifs make Hadklus relatively easy to identify. The decoration of the rest of the field and of the border is made up of small motifs which vary with the tribe that made the rug. One of the most interesting motifs is that used for Hadklu by the Yomut nomads which is vaguely reminiscent of a stylized butterfly. This is a repeating motif which covers the whole field.

The colours of Hadklu rugs are typical of rugs from this region: various shades of red, dark blue and black. In some specimens, the use of white is more pronounced and it serves also as a ground colour.

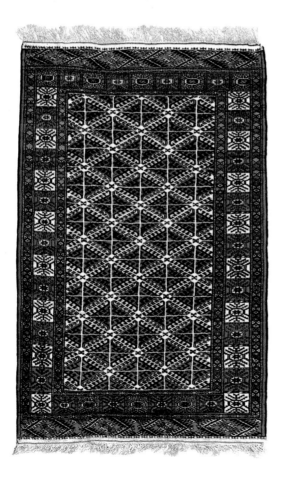

The carpet illustrated on the left is a typical product of the Turkoman tribe of the Yomut. The example illustrated on the opposite page comes from Pakistan. It is decorated with the motif known as Hadklu. The design, originally from Turkestan, is also used in some Pakistani carpets

CHINA

PAZYRYK

Kashgar

Jarkand

Sinkiang

Khotan

Pekin

Tientsin

SAMARKAND

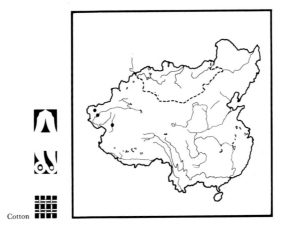

Cotton

PROVENANCE These carpets, too, are known by a name which does not correspond to their place of origin. Samarkand carpets are, in fact, the work of nomadic peoples living in the vast Chinese province of Sinkiang up to the edge of the Sinkiang desert. It is very likely that Samarkand was the eighteenth- and nineteenth-century trading centre for these carpets. The towns nearest to this carpet-making region are: Kashgar, Jarkand and Khotan, all of which are situated in the western part of Sinkiang.

TECHNICAL DETAILS Warp and weft in cotton, except for some rare specimens from the last century which are of wool. There are two or three weft threads between the rows of knots. The pile is always in wool, the Persian knot is used and the density per square inch is quite low: from 25 to 60. The finest specimens come from the Kashgar region.

Samarkand carpets exist in various different sizes but they always tend to be in long shape. The commonest size is 7ft 3in × 11ft 3in.

DESCRIPTION The poor quality of these carpets is betrayed by the low knot density and multiple weft thread. Nevertheless, Samarkand carpets are among the most sought-after and have fetched prices quite as high as those quoted for the more expensive Middle Eastern carpets. This is undoubtedly due to their unrivalled beauty of design and their delicate colour combinations.

Samarkand carpets are decorated in many different ways but have some common characteristics which facilitate identification. Rounded shapes are prevalent in the field design while the border patterns are geometric, with a predominance of the Greek key, especially the one known as running dog.

Very often there is a fairly wide band between the border and the field, and this is decorated solely with rosettes in alternating colours. There are two motifs which occur most frequently in Samarkand field decoration. One consists of three rounded medallions in which there is a form of eight-pointed star, with the points unfolding like the petals of a flower; and in some examples the three medallions' quarters are decorated with a Greek key similar to that used in many Chinese carpets. The other motif typical of Samarkand is a flowering pomegranate tree, an Eastern symbol of plenty, which grows from a vase at the foot of the carpet and covers the whole field. The extraordinary beauty of these specimens results, not just from the decoration, but also from the colour-range: azure and ivory in the field, yellow in the branches and flame in the pomegranates.

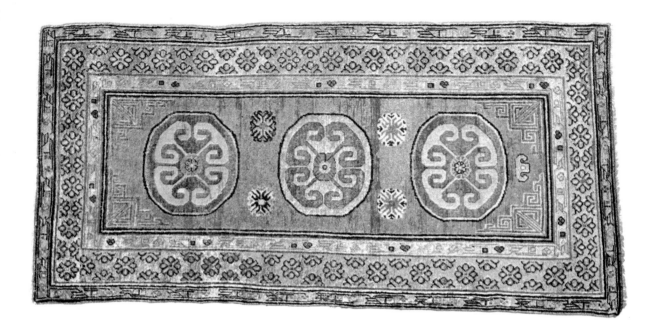

opposite, above: *Classic Samarkand carpet produced in the second half of the eighteenth century. (Private Collection, Milan)*

opposite, below: *Another Samarkand specimen, dating from the nineteenth century, from the centre of Khotan. (Pars Collection, Milan)*

Yet another Samarkand carpet, from the first half of the nineteenth century, decorated with a motif of flowering pomegranate boughs

CHINESE CARPETS

PROVENANCE   Chinese carpets come almost exclusively from large factories in Tientsin and Pekin and from Sinkiang province.

TECHNICAL DETAILS   These are carpets made in large production centres where there are thousands of looms. Although they are still knotted by hand, the work is standardized and hundreds of carpets are made in the same designs and colours.

These carpets are substantially different in character from the Middle East. The warp and weft is in rather thick cotton; the pile is fairly deep and the wool used is extremely soft and shiny – very high quality wool, in fact, though rather delicate.

Another characteristic peculiar to Chinese carpets is the special technique of shearing the pile of the motifs with the result that they stand out much more clearly from the field.

Modern Chinese carpets are divided into different qualities according to the number of lines of knots in a foot and from the different depth of pile. The number of lines of knots per foot may vary between 70 and 90, and the depth of pile from $\frac{3}{8}$ to $\frac{5}{8}$ inches.

The Persian knot is used for Chinese carpets, the knot density being very low – 30 to 60 knots to the square inch.

DESCRIPTION   The decoration of Chinese carpets is divided into two groups: those with a traditional design and those with a Western design.

To the first group belong the carpets which retain links with ancient Chinese carpet-craft. Its chief characteristics are its style and restraint. The colour effect often results from a pleasing combination of blue and a sandy-yellow tone which, together with light blue, turquoise and ivory, is dominant in these carpets. The decoration is simple and consists, for the most part, of various kinds of wavy-line motifs along the edges and a Taoist or Buddhist emblem in the field. Among the most common motifs are: the cloud (chi), the dragon, in different attitudes, the lotus flower, fish, and flower vase.

Chinese carpets with Western motifs are inspired particularly by French Aubusson patterns. The result is a carpet with a sumptuous floral decoration including a magnificent central medallion standing out against a self-colour background and a richly decorated border. The range of background colours is enormous but the motifs are almost exclusively in pastel shades.

Finally, there are the carpets made in the factories of Sinkiang province. Their decoration rings the changes between Caucasian-inspired motifs and others which are typically Chinese.

236

above: *Typical Pekin carpet
woven in the second half of the
nineteenth century*

right: *This carpet, which is
decorated with motifs inspired by
French Aubusson carpets, comes
from Tientsin*

left: *Pekin carpet of modern manufacture. The decorative pattern, however, is a traditional Chinese one*

below: *Specimen from the carpet-making works of Sinkiang*

APPENDICES

MINOR CENTRES

Given below are some other production areas which were not included in the preceding section.

They are small districts or production centres where output is very limited but in all of which a high artistic and technical level has been attained.

AGRA
Generic name given to Indian carpets woven in the nineteenth and early twentieth century. Agra carpets are almost always large.

ALIABAD
Carpets which come from the village of the same name situated near Kashan. The field decoration often consists of herati motifs.

BAKSHAISH
Carpets woven in the village of the same name in the Tabriz area. Both decoration and technical details are similar to those of Heriz carpets.

BRUSSA
Rugs woven in the Turkish town of Brussa. They are usually long prayer rugs with multiple adjoining niches.

CHILA
Rare Caucasian carpets emanating from the Shirvan area. The decoration is typically Caucasian. The colours used for the field are generally rather unusual shades of light and dark blue.

GALTUK
Carpets woven in the area lying between the Hamadan and Arak regions. The decoration is similar to that used for Khamseh carpets.

HEREKE
Rare Turkish carpets woven in the seventeenth and eighteenth centuries in the vicinity of Constantinople.

JOZAN
High quality carpets woven in the village of Jozan near Malayer. The decoration is similar to that of Saruq carpets.

KERMANSHAH
Carpets from the town of the same name in western Iran. The decorative motifs recall those of Hamadan carpets. Kermanshah is also an important collecting point for carpets woven in the neighbouring villages.

KILIM
Characteristic weft-face carpets without a pile. They are embroidered rather than woven, and come from various districts of Anatolia and Iran, particularly Senneh. The techniques used are similar to those of Sumak but with one important difference – the lack of the decorative weft thread.

KUBA OR KABISTAN
Caucasian carpets of the Shirvan family. The most common decoration is made up of lines of rectangles or squares one above the other along the central part of the field. The rest of the field is decorated with a large number of animal figures amongst which the most common is the peacock.

MADHEN
Prayer rugs belonging to the Anatolian group.

MADRAS
Indian carpets woven in Madras towards the end of the nineteenth century.

MEGRI OR MAKRI
Turkish carpets similar to those from Melas. The decoration is often divided into two vertical sections which cover the entire field.

PANDERMA
Carpets from the town of the same name in western Turkey. The very varied decoration contains many Persian designs.

242

SAFF
Characteristic Turkish prayer rugs decorated with multiple niches arranged to form a symmetrical composition which covers the width of the rug. Very often the pile is of silk.

SAVEH
Carpets woven in the agricultural region to the east of Hamadan. They have the same characteristics as Hamadan carpets.

SEICHUR
Caucasian carpets belonging to the Shirvan family. The customary decoration is made up of a repeating design rather like the cross of St Andrew.

TAFRESH
Carpets from the Hamadan region. The technique is of a higher grade than for the generality of work from the area.

TALISH
Caucasian carpets belonging to the Shirvan family. Long shape. Thick pile. The border is simple, often decorated with large rosettes. The field may be plain or divided into squares.

ZABOL
Carpets woven by Baluchi tribes living in the Zabol region (south-east Iran).

ZENJAN
Carpets woven in the villages to the north of Hamadan. The decoration is similar to that used for Khamseh carpets.

BUYING AND MAINTENANCE

BUYING

When purchasing a carpet it is always best to go to a reputable firm. Only the expert is in a position to take into consideration all the factors relating to valuation.

The amateur, however much experience he may have, and however much reading he has done on the subject, will always find himself in difficulties when it comes to judging a carpet.

The most important factors in carpet evaluation are the knot count, the quality of the materials employed – in particular, the quality of the wool used for the pile – the type of dye and the period. It is, however, difficult to estimate the importance of any one of these elements in evaluating the carpet as a whole.

For example, the knot density, the type of design, or the quality of the wool are of varying importance according to where the carpet came from. A carpet with a low knot density might be much more valuable than one of the same period with a high knot density from a different provenance.

It is most important when buying a carpet to make sure that the warp and weft are sound. To be sure of this, all one has to do is to fold the carpet, pile innermost, and jerk the fold slightly. If the carpet creaks, the warp and weft are faulty.

The valuation of a carpet is not, however, based upon empirical criteria but upon very precise current market prices known only to qualified dealers.

A carpet can only be valued by an experienced person who is in daily contact with the carpet market. Therefore, the choice of firm from whom the carpet is to be acquired is of paramount importance. It is advisable only to go to specialist and well-known dealers. A reliable dealer can, even after some time has elapsed, exchange a carpet he has sold if it has, in the meantime, revealed some defect or no longer meets the needs of the purchaser.

It is a good idea to keep clear of bargain and liquidation sales because at these you are much more likely to find yourself with a worthless carpet than with a bargain.

When the time comes to purchase, due consideration must, of course, be given to the eventual setting of the carpet, its size and estimated cost but, in the end, you must let yourself be guided by your own taste. It is far better, for instance, to buy a slightly larger or smaller carpet which you like than a carpet of ideal size which is not entirely satisfying.

MAINTENANCE

By the very nature of their structure and materials, Oriental carpets are very sturdy. Their wearing qualities depend, however, on where they were woven. Normally, the most hard-wearing carpets are those with a cotton warp, a double or treble cotton weft and a medium-depth pile. The most delicate are those made entirely of wool with a single weft thread and a low knot density. For the latter it is advisable to put a pad underneath (the best are made of a layer each of jute and rubber). Besides protecting the carpet from wear, this helps it to lie securely on the floor. Another precaution to be recommended is to use a felt stop under the legs of heavy furniture. In this case, it is also wise to turn the carpet every two or three months to allow the crushed pile to spring back.

If Oriental carpets are treated roughly they will soon deteriorate.

For everyday cleaning it is advisable to use either a brush, or a carpet sweeper. If a brush is used the carpet should be brushed with the pile. The direction of the pile may be discovered by running your hand across the surface of the carpet. For a more thorough cleaning, it is a good idea to run the carpet sweeper three or four times over the back of the carpet until there is no longer a deposit of dust on the floor. After this, run the sweeper over the pile once more.

A carpet beater should never be used because the hard beating may break the warp and weft threads.

SUMMER STORAGE

In hot countries it is customary to store carpets during the summer months to save them from the deteriorating effects of bright light. It is best to go to a specialist firm for this – possibly to the dealer from whom the carpet was purchased – and then the carpet can not only be stored, but also washed under controlled conditions. Small repairs can also be undertaken so that the life and value of the carpet are not impaired. If it is not possible to obtain the services of a specialist firm, the carpet should be sprinkled with a moth-proofing product, rolled up in paper or polythene in the direction of the warp, and stored in a dry place.

WASHING

Carpets should be washed regularly, every year or two according to use. Hand-washing is the best method, being more reliable and giving better results.

When it is not possible to entrust the carpet to a specialist firm, it may be washed at home in a bath, using dilute detergent suitable for washing wool, with a cup of vinegar added. After thorough rinsing the carpet should be left to dry and must be completely dry before it is rolled and stored for the summer.

The best way to wash the fringe is to dip it into a receptacle containing dilute detergent, and then rub.

Stains should be removed as from any wool fabric.

REPAIRS

It is absolutely essential to go to a specialist firm for carpet repairs because a badly executed repair will impair the value of a carpet. The skill and patience of the repairers can perform veritable miracles. It is even possible for a carpet to be put back on a loom for a missing part to be re-woven.

INDEX

BIBLIOGRAPHY

A. Achdjian, *Un art fondamental: le tapis*, Paris, 1949; Bode/Kühnel, *Antique Rugs from the Near East*, London, 1970; R. de Calatchi, *Tapis d'Orient, Histoire, Esthétique, Symbolisme*, Freiburg, 1967; M. Campana, *Tappeti d'Oriente*, Milan, 1966, English edition *CAMEO: Oriental Carpets*, London, 1968; P. M. Campana, *Il tappeto orientale*, Milan, 1962; G. Cohen, *Il fascino del tappeto orientale*, Milan, 1969; A. U. Dilley, *Oriental Rugs and Carpets*, New York, 1959; A. Cecil Edwards, *The Persian Carpet*, London, 1953; H. Haack, *Oriental Rugs*, London, 1960; A. E. Halgeldian, *Tappeti d'Oriente*, Milan, 1959; H. Hildebrand, *Der persische Teppich und seine Heimat*, Zurich, 1951; A Hopf, *Oriental Carpets and Rugs*, London, 1962; L. Kybalová and D. Darbois, *Carpets of the Orient*, London, 1969; A. R. de Leon, *Guide en couleurs du Tapis*, Paris, 1967; J. G. Lettenmair, *Das Grosse Orient-Teppich-Buch*, Munich, 1962; P. Liebetran, *Orientalske Toepper i Farver*, Copenhagen, 1962; F. R. Martin, *A History of Oriental Carpets before 1800*, Vienna, 1908; F. Mazzini, *Tappeti orientali*, Leghorn, 1942; A. U. Pope, *A Survey of Persian Art*, London and New York, 1938–1939; H. Ropers, *Les Tapis d'Orient*, Paris, 1958; F. Sarre and H. Trenkwald, *Anciens Tapis d'Orient* (2 vols.) Leipzig, Vienna, Paris, 1927–1929; I. Schlosser, *Tapis d'Orient et d'Occident*, Freiburg, 1962; U. Tolomei, *Il tappeto orientale*, Novara, 1968; M. and V. Viale, *Arazzi et tappeti antichi*, Turin, 1952.

PHOTOGRAPHIC CREDITS

Except for those mentioned below, all the photographs in this volume are by Gaio Bacci, Carmelo Balzarini and Pino Dal Gal.

Mario De Biasi: 55, 60; J. R. Freeman, Victoria & Albert Museum, London: 30, 32; Isaac D. Fletcher Collection, bequest of Isaac D. Fletcher, 1917, The Metropolitan Museum of Art, New York: 41; Kungl. Vitterhets Histoire och Antikvitets Akademien (Stockholm): 28; The Hermitage, Leningrad: 15; F. A. Mella, National Gallery, London: 6; Poldi Pezzoli Museum, Milan: 34; Walter Mori: 48–49, 53 left and right, 62–63, 247; H. Prüstel © Holle Verlag, Baden-Baden 1964: 14; E. Ritter, Österreichisches Museum für angewandte Kunst, Vienna: 37, 43, 45; Studio GES, Verona: 70, 71, 72, 73, 74, 75, 76, 77, 78, 79; A. J. Wyatt, The Philadelphia Museum of Art, Williams Collection, Philadelphia: 39.

The sketches are by Studio GES, Verona.